E. G. Stephenson

April 9, 1912.

Riverby Edition

THE WRITINGS OF
JOHN BURROUGHS

WITH PORTRAITS AND MANY ILLUSTRATIONS

VOLUME XI

THE WRITINGS

OF

JOHN BURROUGHS

XI

THE LIGHT OF DAY

RELIGIOUS DISCUSSIONS AND CRITICISMS FROM
THE NATURALIST'S POINT OF VIEW

BOSTON AND NEW YORK
HOUGHTON MIFFLIN COMPANY
The Riverside Press Cambridge

WAITING

Serene, I fold my hands and wait,
  Nor care for wind, nor tide, nor sea;
I rave no more 'gainst Time or Fate,
  For lo! my own shall come to me.

I stay my haste, I make delays,
  For what avails this eager pace?
I stand amid the eternal ways,
  And what is mine shall know my face.

Asleep, awake, by night or day,
  The friends I seek are seeking me;
No wind can drive my bark astray,
  Nor change the tide of destiny.

What matter if I stand alone?
  I wait with joy the coming years;
My heart shall reap where it hath sown,
  And garner up its fruit of tears.

The waters know their own, and draw
  The brook that springs in yonder heights;
So flows the good with equal law
  Unto the soul of pure delights.

The stars come nightly to the sky;
  The tidal wave comes to the sea;
Nor time, nor space, nor deep, nor high,
  Can keep my own away from me.

PREFACE

In Central Asia, near the river Oxus, there is said to be a famous rock, called the Lamp Rock, from a strange light that seems to issue from a cavern far up on the side of the mountain. The natives have a superstitious fear of the rock, and ascribe the light to some dragon or demon that lives in the cave. Recently a bold English traveler climbed up and investigated the phenomenon. The light was found, after all, to be only the light of common day. The cave proved to be a tunnel, and the mysterious light came through the rock from the other side, making a strong glow or nimbus at the mouth of the dark cavern.

This incident, so typical of much that has taken place and is still taking place in the world, especially in the religious experience of mankind, has suggested the title to this volume of essays, in which I have urged the sufficiency and the universality of natural law, and that most of the mysterious lights with which our fears, our ignorance, or our superstitions have invested the subject of religion, when brought to the test of reason, either vanish entirely or give place to the light of common day.

PREFACE

The essays for the most part were written twelve or fifteen years ago, when the author's mind was more under the spell of these and kindred subjects than it is at present. They are reprinted now under the belief that they have sufficient merit, literary and other, to warrant such a course.

Written at different times and for different occasions, it is perhaps inevitable that they should show more or less repetition. Certain channels were, so to speak, worn in my mind by the consideration of these matters, and that a like experience may not befall the reader, I advise him to read no more than one chapter at a single sitting.

My polemic, so far as it is such, will be found, I hope, aimed more at theology than at religion. Theology passes; religion, as a sentiment or feeling of awe and reverence in the presence of the vastness and mystery of the universe, remains. The old theology had few if any fast colors, and it has become very faded and worn under the fierce light and intense activity of our day. Let it go; it is outgrown and outworn. What mankind will finally clothe themselves with to protect them from the chill of the great void, or whether or not they will clothe themselves at all, but become toughened and indifferent, is more than I can pretend to say. For my own part, the longer I live, the less I feel the need of any sort of theological belief, and the more I am content to let the unseen powers go their own

PREFACE

way with me and mine without question or distrust. They brought me here, and I have found it well to be here; in due time they will take me hence, and I have no doubt that will be well for me too.

We are like figures which some great demonstrator draws upon the blackboard of Time. A problem is to be solved, without doubt; what the problem is, we, the figures, cannot know and do not need to know; all we know is that sooner or later we shall be sponged off the board and other figures take our places, and the demonstration go on.

That we have served a purpose, that we have positively appeared, that something has been fulfilled in us — is not that enough? To have played a part with other figures, and to leave the board clear for other forms that are to embody higher results and more far-reaching conclusions — is not that enough?

April, 1900.

CONTENTS

LIST OF ILLUSTRATIONS

difference of views between them, and begin to quote his texts. Trumps called for trumps, and father could match every one of Jerry's texts with one of his own. Jerry was the more ready and smooth of tongue, but I think father had the greater depth of religious feeling. I can see him now as he sat with the Book open on his knees, a tallow dip in his hand, his face flushed, his voice loud, hurling Paul's predestinarianism at his neighbor's free salvation Methodism. Back and forth the disputants, like two fencers, fought the ground over. Sometimes one clearly had the advantage, sometimes a telling text gave it to the other. Both looked upon the Bible as the infallible Word of God, but neither took it in a " soft and flexible sense," to use the words of Sir Thomas Browne, but in a rigid, dogmatic sense. Both were, or thought they were, God-fearing men, but each looked upon the religious belief of the other with the utmost contempt. The sect to which my father belonged was especially narrow and harsh in its judgments of other sects, particularly of the Methodists, who on nearly all points were exactly their antipodes. The name of Methodism, with its cheap and easy terms of salvation, always made father's lip curl and his nostrils dilate. He would not have been caught in one of their churches on any account whatever.

The old school Baptists look upon themselves as the elect, the chosen few, the remnant that is to be saved, and they treat all other claimants to an interest in the Celestial City as pretenders. It was to bring them forth that the whole creation groaned and travailed in pain all the ages. How they snort at divinity schools, Sunday-schools, missionaries, protracted meetings, paid and educated clergymen, and prepared sermons. Only he who is called of God can preach (how true!), and he shall take no thought of what he is to say until he gets into the pulpit. Hence the sermons I frequently listened to in my youth, that were supposed to be the direct inspiration of the Creator of heaven and earth, were of a kind to make Blair turn gray in an hour. But how can the carnal mind understand these things!

I am bound to say that the God of our neighbor was a more benevolent and merciful God than the one my father believed in. He wanted all to be saved, whether they would be or not, while the other had carefully provided that only a part could or should be saved.

The disputants of course never succeeded in changing each other's views, but only in causing them to be held more tenaciously. They both as old men died in the faith they had early professed. It was sufficient unto them while they lived, and at the last it did not fail them. Father always spoke of his approaching end with perfect assurance and composure. He looked upon it as some journey he was about to make, some change of scene that was to come to him, and which need give him none but happy anticipation. I remember that once while visiting him, a few years before his death, he told me he was reading the Bible through again. He had just been reading the story of Elijah and the false prophets. He told me the story, and when he came to where the fire came down from heaven and consumed Elijah's offering, his emotion overcame him, and he broke down completely. He no more doubted these things, he no more doubted the literal truth of every passage in the Bible, than he did his own existence.

How impossible for me to read the Bible as father or Jerry did, or to feel any interest in the questions which were so vital to them; not because I have hardened my heart against these things, but mainly because I was born forty years later than they were, with different tastes and habits of mind. The time spirit has wrought many changes in men's views, and I have seen the world with other eyes and through other mediums.

II

FROM THE ARTIFICIAL TO THE NATURAL

FROM the first the progress of mankind has been slowly but surely from the artificial to the natural, from the arbitrary and chimerical to the simple and scientific. Getting himself and his affairs more and more into natural currents and following them — this is the way man has progressed.

All early peoples and savage tribes have extremely arbitrary and artificial notions of the world of forces amid which they live. The more they are immersed in brute nature, the more unnatural will be their practices and conceptions. People who live in a state of nature are the victims of delusions and superstitions.

Nearly all the early conceptions of the universe that have come down to us are artificial. The Mosaic account of creation shows God a literal maker and builder, Heaven and Hell mere *places*, one above and the other beneath the earth. The Ptolemaic system of astronomy shows how artificial was the beginning of this science. The conception which the early Christian fathers had of the universe was that it was foursquare like Solomon's temple, and that the sky was something fastened to the outer edges.

The ancient cities were built or made in a sense that ours are not. They did not grow. They were deliberately designed and built as we build a house, — Jerusalem, Tyre, Sidon, Carthage, Athens, Rome, Paris, London, were not the result of natural laws and forces, working through commerce or the spontaneous movements of peoples, as are modern cities, but the result of arbitrary power.

All political progress has been the removal of forced and artificial relations among men, and the establishment of natural relations. Democracy is a search for natural leaders and the rights and privileges that belong to man by virtue of his manhood. There is much that is still arbitrary in American politics and sociology. The new movement, nationalism, is a revolt against these conditions.

It is doubtful if any of the unnatural crimes and vices of the ancient world prevail to any considerable extent to-day.

What progress in medicine from the artificial to the natural, from the chimerical to the scientific! The early remedies were nearly all fantastic, like Indian medicine in our own time. The Indian makes a tea of tickseed, or beggar's lice, to improve the memory ; it will make things *stick* to you.

8

The doctrine of " signatures," which at one time exercised such an influence on medicine, was just as rational. The plant called Jew's ear was used as a remedy for diseases of the ear, because its shape was somewhat like that organ. Liver leaf, I suppose, would cure liver troubles for a similar reason. The dried flesh of the python was a great remedy, also powdered mummy. A hundred other remedies were equally fantastic.

The first or earliest conception of disease was that it was the result of an evil spirit, and it was to be exorcised or driven away by some religious rite or ceremony. The priests were therefore the first doctors. The spirit theory of disease was long since abandoned, but the spirit theory of insanity, or demoniacal possession, is still held by some of our doctors of divinity. The president of a New England college not long since stated his belief in this doctrine.

Up to near the end of the first half of our own century, our system of medicine was as artificial as our theology. The doctor abhorred nature about as much as the priest did. The latter taught that man was saved by grace, not by any virtue or excellence in himself, and the doctor taught that disease was cured by drugs, not by any recuperative power in the body. But drugs and nostrums are in our day at a discount. The doctor no longer aims to suppress symptoms, but to remove causes. His chief reliance is upon nature, fresh air, water, exercise, correct habits, proper food, etc. He does not try to stop a fever but to guide it, and keep up the strength of the patient.

In religion the progress has been precisely like that in medicine, — from the arbitrary, the fantastic, to the simple and the natural; from the conception of a universe the sport and tool of supernatural beings, to a world inexorably bound by the sequence of cause and effect, or like that from the Ptolemaic astronomy to the Copernican system. That the early religions were fantastic and unreal needs no proof. That the Christian mythology is equally fantastic and unreal is not so generally admitted. The teachings of Jesus himself were simple and natural in the extreme, but out of the notions which were formed *about* Jesus there grew up a religious organization which was equally the extreme of complexity and artificiality. For seventeen hundred years mankind were under its sway as under a nightmare. It perverted nearly every natural fact, and paralyzed nearly every natural instinct of the heart. In the Catholic Church this nightmare still rides mankind; in the Protestant churches its spell has been partially broken. Protestantism is more or less a compromise with reason, but Catholicism deliberately puts reason under foot. The Catholic reasons very astutely within certain limits, but he is tethered and cannot go beyond a fixed point. His reason is the

10

servant of his faith and obeys it implicitly. It is like a muzzled ferret, that hunts not for itself but for its master; the game belongs to faith.

The priest with his magic and the doctor with his nostrums have had their day. If natural goodness will not save a man, he is lost, and if his innate powers of recuperation will not cure him, he must die, just as has always been the case.

III

SCIENCE AND THEOLOGY

ONE of the latest phases of the religious thought of the times seems to be a desire to get rid of, or to explain away, the supernatural, — at least to reclaim and domesticate it and convince mankind that it is not the irresponsible outlaw we have so long been led to suppose, — a desire nearly as marked in the theology as in the science of the day. Thus, the Bishop of Exeter (Dr. Temple), in his Bampton Lectures of 1884, on the "Relations between Religion and Science," upholds the belief in miracles, without calling to his aid the belief in the supernatural as the word is commonly used. A miracle, he urges, *may* be only some phase of the natural not yet understood ; the turning of water into wine by word of command, or the miracle of the loaves and the fishes, may have been accomplished by the exercise of some power over nature which is perfectly scientific, but of which man as yet has imperfect control.

And the Duke of Argyll, in his "Reign of Law," cautions us against assigning an event or a phenomenon to the agency of the supernatural until we are quite sure we understand the limits of the natural, — the natural may reach far enough to include all that we have commonly called the supernatural. The latest considerable attempt in this direction is furnished by the work of Professor Henry Drummond on " Natural Law in the Spiritual World," a work which undertakes to demonstrate the naturalness of the supernatural, or the oneness of religion and biology.

Butler, in his " Analogy," says that there is no " absurdity in supposing that there may be beings in the universe whose capacity and knowledge and views may be so extensive as that the whole Christian dispensation may to them appear natural; that is, analogous or conformable to God's dealings with other parts of his creation; as natural as the visible known course of things appear to us."

Such a being seems actually to have appeared in the person of this Scotch professor. The " whole Christian dispensation " is to him little more than a question of experimental science ; the conversion of Paul is as natural and explicable a process to him as the hatching of an egg or the sprouting of a kernel of corn. " Religion," he says, " is no disheveled mass of aspiration, prayer, and faith. There is no more mystery in religion as to its process than in biology." The question of a future life is only a biological problem to him. He gives physiological tests by which a man may surely know whether or not he is a true Christian. The characteristics of life in the organic world, he argues, are four : namely, assimilation, waste, reproduction, and spontaneous action ; the characteristics in the Christian world are the same ; *must* be the same, else the law of continuity, upon which he has built, fails. But he wisely refrains from applying these tests in detail to the spiritual life of the Christian. He says : "The experiment would be a delicate one. It might not be open to every one to attempt it. This is a scientific question; and the experiment would have to be conducted under proper conditions and by competent persons."

There is little mystery in the universe to a mind like Drummond's ; or if there is any mystery, he knows exactly what and where it is; he has cornered and labeled it, so that it shall give him no further trouble.

We hardly need the confession which he makes in his preface, that his science and his religion have got so thoroughly mixed that either can be expressed in the terms of the other. For a time, he says (while he was teaching the two, one on week days, the other on Sundays), he succeeded in keeping them shut off from one another in two separate "compartments" of his mind. "But gradually the wall of partition showed symptoms of giving way. The two fountains of knowledge also slowly began to overflow, and finally their waters met and mingled.

15

The great change was in the compartment which held the religion. It was not that the well there was dried; still less that the fermenting waters were washed away by the flood of science. The actual contents remained the same. But the crystals of former doctrines were dissolved ; and, as they precipitated themselves over more indefinite forms, I observed that the Crystalline System was changed. New channels for outward expression opened, and some of the old closed up ; and I found the truth running out to my audience on Sundays by the week-day outlets."

It is but fair to say that this extract does not show our professor's style at its best, but rather at its worst. At its worst it is grossly materialistic, and goes in the leading-strings of a cheap and overwrought analogy. At its best it is often singularly clear and forcible, even flexible and buoyant, but it always wants delicacy and spirituality, and appeals to the scientific rather than to the religious sense. But a more confused mixture of science and theology probably the whole range of printed books does not afford. The positions and conclusions of the latter are constantly uttered as if they were the demonstrations of the former. And this is the obnoxious feature of the book. With Professor Drummond's theology, as such, I have nothing to do, having long ago made my peace with Calvinism. It is only because he utters his theology in the name of science, or as the result of a scientific demonstration, that I am occupied with him here.

When it is declared by a college professor of Natural Science, as it virtually is in this book, that in the laws and processes of the physical universe that which is science at one end is Scotch Presbyterianism at the other, the proposition arrests attention by its novelty at least.

"The spiritual world as it stands," he declares, "is full of perplexity. One can escape doubt only by escaping thought. . . . The old ground of faith, authority, is given up; the new [ground], science, has not taken its place." It is his purpose to give to faith this new ground of science. Up to this time, he says, the spiritual world has been looked upon as outside of natural law. Evolution and revelation have been at swords' points; he has not merely made peace between them, but he clearly believes himself to have enlisted the forces of the former under the banner of the latter. Science, he says, can hear nothing of a "Great Exception." The present decadence of religion is owing to the fact that it has been too long treated as the great exception,—cut off by an insurmountable barrier from the natural order of things. It is now found by this Christian philosopher to be as completely under the dominion of natural law as any branch of physical science. What Jussieu and De Candolle did for botany in substituting the natural system for the

17

artificial, what Lyell did for geology in getting rid of "catastrophism," what Newton did for astronomy by his law of gravitation, our Glasgow professor flatters himself (rather covertly, to be sure) he has done, or showed the way to do, for theology. He has introduced law and order where before were chaos and "perplexity."

All this sounds as promising to the man of science as it must sound bewildering and discouraging to the theologian, — because, has not theology always maintained that revealed religion was superior to reason, and that the natural man, with his profane sciences, was at enmity with God?

Sir Thomas Browne speaks as a theologian when he says that reason is a rebel unto faith, and that "many things are true in divinity which are neither inducible by reason nor confirmable by sense;" but he spoke as a man of science when he said: "I can cure vices by physic when they remain incurable by divinity; and they shall obey my pills when they contemn their precepts." Indeed, science and divinity occupy essentially different points of view, in many respects antagonistic points of view.

Science, in the broadest sense, is simply that which may be verified; but how much of that which theology accepts and goes upon is verifiable by human reason or experience? The kind of evidence which theology accepts, or has accepted in the past, is too much like that which led the old

18

astrologer Nostradamus to predict the end of the world in 1886, because in this year Good Friday falls upon St. George's day, and Easter upon St. Mark's day, the very latest date upon which Easter can happen.

Theology, for the most part, adopts the personal point of view, — the point of view of our personal wants, fears, hopes, weaknesses, and shapes the universe with man as the centre. It has no trouble to believe in miracles, because miracles show the triumph of the personal element over impersonal law. Its strongest hold upon the mind of the race was in the pre-scientific age. It is the daughter of mythology, and has made the relation of the unseen powers to man quite as intimate and personal. It looks upon this little corner of the universe as the special theatre of the celestial powers, — powers to whom it has given the form and attributes of men, and to whom it ascribes curious plans and devices. Its point of view is more helpful and sustaining to the mass of mankind than that of science ever can be, because the mass of mankind are children, and are ruled by their affections and their emotions. Science chills and repels them, because it substitutes a world of force and law for a world of humanistic divinities.

Of all the great historical religions of the world, theology sees but one to be true and of divine origin; all the rest are of human invention, and for the most part mere masses of falsehood and superstition. Science recognizes the religious instinct in man as a permanent part of his nature, and looks upon the great systems of religion — Christianity, Judaism, Buddhism, Mohammedanism, the polytheism of Greece, Rome, and Egypt — as its legitimate outgrowth and flowering, just as much as the different floras and faunas of the earth are the expression of one principle of organic life. All these religions may be treated as false, or all of them treated as true; what we cannot say, speaking for science, is, that one is true and all the others are false. To it they are all false with reference to their machinery, but all true with reference to the need to which they administer. They are like the constellations of the astronomical maps, wherein the only things that are true and real are the stars; all the rest — Ursa Major, Cassiopeia, Orion, etc. — are the invention of the astronomers. The eternal truths of man's religious nature have lent themselves to many figures of polytheism as well as of Christianity; these figures pass away or become discredited, but the truths themselves — the recognition of a Power greater and wiser than ourselves, to the law of which it is necessary that our conduct in some measure conform — never pass away. Was not Egypt saved by her religion, and Greece by hers, as much as England is by hers?

Indeed, the question which it is not safe to ask of

any religion is just the one we are prone to ask first, namely, Is it true? A much safer question is, Is it saving? That is, does it hold men up to a higher standard of life and duty than they were otherwise capable of? Does it cheer and sustain them in their journey through this world? Could the religion of Greece have faced the question, Is it true? And yet the German historian of Greece, Dr. Curtius, says that the religion of Apollo " was nowhere introduced without taking hold of and transforming the whole life of the people. It liberated men from dark and groveling worship of Nature; it converted the worship of a god into the duty of moral elevation; it founded expiations for those oppressed with guilt, and for those astray, without guidance, sacred oracles." Can historical Christianity any better face the question, Is it true? Did all these events fall out as set down in the New Testament? Are they set in their true light? And yet who besides Professor Clifford dare say that Christianity has not been a tremendous power in elevating and civilizing the European nations?

Science affirms that every child born of woman since the world began belonged to the human species, and had an earthly father; theology affirms that this is true of every child but one: one child, born in Judea over eighteen hundred years ago, was an exception, was indeed very God himself. Theology makes a similar claim with regard to the Bible. It

affirms that every book in the world was written by
a human being, and is therefore more or less fallible
and imperfect, with the exception of one — that one
is the Bible. This is the great exception: the Bible
is not the work of man, but is the word of God
himself uttered through man, and is therefore infallible. Science simply sees in the Bible one of the
sacred books of the nations,—undoubtedly the greatest of them all, — but still a book or a collection of
books embodying the history, the ideas, the religious
wants and yearnings of a very peculiar people, — a
people without a vestige of science, but with the tie
of race and the aspiration after God stronger than
in any people, — a people still wandering in the
wilderness, and rejected by the nations to whom
they gave Christianity. Science knows God, too, as
law, or as the force and vitality which pervade and
uphold all things; it knows Jesus as a great teacher
and prophet, and as the Saviour of men. How?
By virtue of the contract made in the Council of
the Trinity as set forth in the creed of Calvinism?
No; but by his unique and tremendous announce-
ment of the law of love, and the daily illustration of
it in his life. Salvation by Jesus is salvation by self-
renunciation, and by gentleness, mercy, charity,
purity, and by all the divine qualities he illustrated.
He saves us when we are like him, — as tender, as
charitable, as unworldly, as devoted to principle,
as self-sacrificing. His life and death do inspire in

mankind these things ; fill them with this noble
ideal. He was a soul impressed, as perhaps no other
soul ever had been, with the oneness of man with
God, and that the kingdom of heaven is not a
place, but a state of mind. Hence, coming to Jesus
is coming to our truer, better selves, and conform-
ing our lives to the highest ideal. Was not Paul a
Saviour of mankind also ? Without Paul it is probable that Christianity would have cut but an insig-
nificant figure in this world. He was its thunder-
bolt; his words still tingle in our ears.

I by no means say that this is the only view that
can be taken of Jesus as the Saviour of mankind;
I say it is the only view science or reason can take,
— the only view which is in harmony with the rest
of our knowledge of the world.

What can science, or, if you please, the human
reason, in its quest of exact knowledge, make of the
cardinal dogmas of the Christian Church, — the plan
of salvation, justification, the Trinity, or "saving
grace," etc. ? Simply nothing. These things were
to the Jews a stumbling-block and to the Greeks
foolishness, and to the man of science they are like
an utterance in an unknown tongue. He has no
means of verifying them ; they lie in a region entirely beyond his ken.

Witness the efforts of the Andover professors, in
their latest manifesto, " Progressive Orthodoxy," to
give a basis of reason to the dogma of vicarious

atonement. The result is mere verbal jugglery. To say that Jesus, laying down his life, makes you or me, or any man *capable* of repenting in a way or in a degree we were not capable of before, or that a man's capacity in any direction can be increased without effort on his part, and by an event of which he may never have heard, are assertions not credible, because they break completely with the whole system of natural knowledge.

In short, the truth of this whole controversy between science and theology seems to me to be this: If we take science as our sole guide, if we accept and hold fast that alone which is verifiable, the old theology, with all its miraculous machinery, must go. But if there is a higher principle by which we are to be guided in religious matters, if there is an eye of faith which is superior to the eye of reason, — a proposition which I here neither affirm nor deny, — then the whole aspect of the question is changed, and it is science and not theology that is blocking the way.

But the attitude of Professor Drummond is that there is nothing true in divinity that is not true in science, or at least in harmony with science, and the main purpose of his book is to demonstrate this.

The proof here offered is nothing more than the old argument from analogy, the analogy being drawn from the principles of biology instead of from the general course of nature, as with Butler. It is the assumption that these biological processes or laws are identical in the spiritual and physical spheres that furnishes the starting-point of the book. "The position we have been led to take up is not that the spiritual laws are analogous to the natural laws, but that they *are the same laws*. It is not a question of analogy, but of *identity*." Still, the identity is not proved; the analogy alone is apparent. In the physical sphere science often recognizes the same laws appearing under widely different conditions. For instance, the process by which animal life is kept up is no doubt a real combustion, identical in kind with that which takes place in the consumption of fuel by fire. Lavoisier and Laplace long ago taught us that there are not two chemistries, one for dead bodies and another for living. On the contrary, one system of laws, chemical, mechanical, physical, everywhere prevails. Again, there are few exact terms that we apply to objective nature that we do not apply upon the principle of analogy to subjective nature, as high and low, interior and exterior, flexible and inflexible, hard and soft, attraction and repulsion. Indeed, our whole language, in its higher ranges, is a perpetual application of the principle of analogy. But to aver that physical laws are operative in the spiritual world, even in the spiritual world of Calvinistic theology, is quite another matter, and is to take a leap where science cannot follow. Hard and inflexible as the Calvinistic

prove the doctrine of the resurrection of the body. He appealed to a perfectly natural and familiar phenomenon, namely, the decay and transformation of a kernel of wheat in the ground before it gives birth to the stalk and the new grain. But see how the doctrine which he maintained so eloquently has faded, or is fading, from the mind of even orthodox Christendom! Analogy is valuable as rhetoric, but in the serious pursuit of truth it can be of little service to us. When employed for its argumentative force, it proceeds upon the theory that if two things be compared, a matter in question with a matter about which there can be no question, and the former be found to agree in its *rationale* with the latter, the presumption is that it is true as the latter is true. But this mode of reasoning is of no value in religious matters, because here we shape the unknown from our knowledge of the known, and the agreement between the two is already assured. The world of myth and fable bears a resemblance more or less striking to the real world, but does that afford any ground for our accepting the myths and fables as actual facts and occurrences?

Suppose the doctrine of Christian conversion, as expounded by Paul, is found to agree with certain well-known and universal facts of human life, does that prove the doctrine to be true? Or does it prove that Paul predicated his doctrine upon the knowledge of these facts? Milton's rebellious angels in their warfare against the hosts of heaven may not violate one rule of good English military tactics, but that fact would hardly be counted sufficient evidence for our accepting the rebellion as an actual historical event. Indeed, when our theological friends ask us to accept their dogmas on the ground that they are no more unreasonable or inexplicable than many things which we do believe, and which all the world believes, they usually make the mistake of expecting us to award the same weight to the argument from analogy that we do to proof from experience.

That a thing is mysterious or inexplicable affords no grounds for our refusing to credit it. We cannot explain the simplest facts of our lives; we are embosomed in mystery. We do not know how our food nourishes us, or how our sleep refreshes us, yet we know that they *do* nourish and refresh us, and that is enough. What a mystery that an ugly worm should become a gorgeous butterfly, or that from a little insensate egg should come a bird with all its powers of flight and song! How wonderful and inexplicable are the commonest facts and occurrences about us! Yet we know that things do turn out thus and thus and not otherwise, and we know it not from reason but by experience. We know that a man may survive the amputation of his arms and legs, but do we know that he can survive the amputation of his head? A tree or a cabbage survives the amputation of its head ; the stump will sprout again, why not a man ? It is not a matter of reason, I say again, but of experience. When the doctrine of the Trinity can be confirmed by the same test, then it will be just as easy to believe it true as it is that water flows or is solid according to the temperature. The difficulty with the theologians is that, while they so often appeal to our experience in establishing their premises, they at once go beyond our experience in drawing their conclusions.

The analogy upon which Professor Drummond builds so confidently will be found comforting and reassuring to those who are already of his creed, but to the disinterested inquirer, determined to hold fast alone to that which is verifiable, it is little more than a clever rhetorical flourish.

His argument in a nutshell is this: There are three kingdoms, — the inorganic, the organic, and the spiritual, — each atop of the other, and carrying the same law into higher regions. There may be other kingdoms, he says, higher in the scale than the spiritual, or the kingdom of God, of which we as yet know nothing. But of these three we do know, and with these we have to deal. The law of evolution works in each one of these kingdoms up to a certain point, when there is a break, and miracle or an outside power steps in. There is no passage from the inorganic to the organic without a miracle, and no passage from the natural to the spiritual without a miracle. Evolution worked in the nebulous matter till the worlds were formed and ready for life: to introduce that life, God did directly step in by a creative act. This done, evolution went to work again and carried forward the process until the series of sentient beings was crowned by man. Then evolution came to the end of its tether again; to reach the spiritual kingdom the intervention of a miraculous power was again required. A man can no more become a Christian by his own will or act than the inorganic can become the organic. *He cannot* — the thing is simply impossible; and our author brings Scriptural texts to support his position. This leads him into good old-fashioned Calvinism, and good old-fashioned Calvinism he advocates and seeks to clinch with his scientific hammer. Indeed, his aim is to lend the great authority of science to this all but outgrown creed, and he evidently flatters himself that he has established the truth of it beyond all question. The reader soon perceives that the spiritual world of which he is all the while talking is not the spiritual world of the rest of mankind, — the world of spirit as opposed to that of matter, the world of mind and consciousness of which all men are more or less partakers by virtue of their humanity, — but the spiritual world as interpreted by a certain Christian sect, a very limited and a very recent affair, of which the mass of mankind have never even heard, and in which the sages and prophets of antiquity have no part nor lot. The curious and astonishing thing about the argument is, not the bringing forward and the insisting upon this kind of a spiritual world, for theology has long ago made us familiar with this claim, but the bringing of it forward in the name of science and substituting it for the spiritual world which science really recognizes. In following his argument one constantly feels the ground disappearing beneath him or before him. His spiritual kingdom does not belong to the same order of fact as the other two: it is not a link, or a step in a natural series, but a domain by itself entirely apart from human reason or experience. Clapping it on top of the physical universe in the way it has been done here, and claiming that its position there is logical or scientific, is to do violence to common sense. Its position there is forced and arbitrary. In the order of nature, what goes atop of the animal world is the world of consciousness, the world of mind and spirit, which attains to its full flowering in man. This is no limited or accidental world, thrust upon the few, and denied to the many, but a world which belongs to the natural order of the universe. The passage to it from the animal is so gradual that science cannot say where the one ends and the other begins. In the same manner the animal fades into the vegetable, and the vegetable into the mineral. There are no breaks, there are no gulfs fixed. "There exists no insurmountable chasm between organic and inorganic nature," says Haeckel, speaking for the most thorough science of his times. Huxley and Tyndall and the leading French scientists have reached the same conclusion. The organic and the inorganic are composed of the same elements; their differences arise solely from the different chemical combination of these elements, a combination so peculiar and complex that Science has not yet been able to reproduce it in her laboratory. But the fact that spontaneous generation has not yet taken place under the highly artificial conditions imposed by experimental chemistry proves what? Proves only that it has not yet taken place, that science with its limited means and brief space of time has not yet accomplished that which must have occurred under vastly different conditions in the abysm of geological time, and in the depths of the primordial seas. Science starts with matter and with force; back of these it does not go; more than these it does not require. To account for them, or to seek to account for them, is unscientific, for the simple reason that no such accounting can be verified. Out of the potencies of matter itself science traces the evolution of the whole order of visible things. Theology may step in and assume to know all that science leaves unsaid, but in doing so, let it not assume to speak with the consent and the authority of its great rival.

SCIENCE AND THEOLOGY

In the light of the most advanced biological science, organic and inorganic appear but relative terms, like heat and cold. There are all degrees of heat, and there are probably all degrees of life. There are probably degrees of life too low in the scale for our discernment, just as there is heat where our senses report only cold. If there are degrees of consciousness, why may there not be degrees of life? The child grows gradually into consciousness, just as the race has grown gradually into consciousness. Dare we affirm that in either case the leap from the unconscious to the conscious was or is suddenly made? No more dare we affirm that the leap from the inorganic to the organic was suddenly made. Is the crystal absolutely dead? See it shape itself according to a special plan; see how sensitive it is to the surrounding medium; see it grow when the proper food is given it, so to speak. Pasteur has noted that it cicatrizes or repairs itself when wounded. When placed in the fluid of crystallization, the injured part sears over and gradually regains its original shape. The most advanced science of our time does not regard life as a special and separate principle, a real entity which has been added to matter, but as a mode in which certain physical forces manifest themselves, just as heat is not a thing of itself, but a mode of motion.

"Mechanical, chemical, and physical forces are the only efficient agents in the living organism," at least the only ones which science can recognize, and these forces are the same in both the organic and the inorganic worlds.

Behold a fire, a conflagration; see it leap and climb; witness its fierce activity, its all-devouring energies! How like a thing of life it is! Is there a unique and original principle at work here, the principle or spirit of fire, a thing apart from the intense chemical activity which it occasions? The ancient observers believed so, and it is a pretty fancy, but science recognizes in it only another of the protean forms in which force clothes itself. We can evoke fire without the aid of fire, but the fire called life man has not yet been able so to evoke, — probably never will be able. The nearest he has as yet come to it is in producing many of the organic compounds synthetically from inorganic compounds, — a triumph a few years ago thought to be impossible.

The barrier, then, between the organic and the inorganic, upon which the scheme of theology of Professor Drummond turns, is by no means a fixed conclusion of science. Science believes that the potencies or properties of life are on the inorganic side, and that the passage has actually taken place in the past or may still take place in the present.

In working out his general thesis, our author takes courage from the example of Walter Bagehot, whose physical politic, he says, is but the extension of natural law to the political world ; and from the example of Herbert Spencer, whose biological soci- ology is but the application of natural law to the social world. But the political world of Walter Bagehot and the social world of Herbert Spencer are worlds which science recognizes ; they fall within its pale; their existence is never disputed. But the spiritual world of Professor Drummond is a world of which science can know nothing. It is to science just as fanciful or unreal as the spiritual world of Grecian or Scandinavian mythology, or as the fairy world of childhood.

It is true the world of art, the world of genius, the world of literature, is a very select and limited affair too; but does anybody ever call the reality of it in question ? Do we want proof that Shakespeare and Milton are poets ? But science does want proof, if the matter comes to that, that the typical Puritan has the favor of any spiritual powers not known to the rest of mankind, — not known and equally accessible to Zeno or Plutarch or Virgil or Marcus Aurelius.

It is just these exceptions, these departures from the established course of nature, that the natural philosopher is skeptical about. If an obscure event, which happened in Judea over eighteen hundred years ago, added a new kingdom to nature, or in- augurated a new or higher order of spiritual truths impossible before that time, impossible to Plato or

Plutarch, he wants the fact put in harmony with the rest of our knowledge of the universe. It is commonly believed that the course of nature is independent of historical events, and that the ways of God to man from the beginning have been just what they are to-day.

What perpetually irritates the disinterested reader of Drummond's book is the assumption everywhere met with that the author is speaking with the authority of science, when he is only echoing the conclusions of theology. Hear him on the differences between the Christian and the non-Christian : —

"The distinction between them is the same as that between the organic and the inorganic, the living and the dead. What is the difference between a crystal and an organism, a stone and a plant? They have much in common. Both are made of the same atoms. Both display the same properties of matter. Both are subject to the same physical laws. Both may be very beautiful. But besides possessing all that the crystal has, the plant possesses something more, — a mysterious something called life. This life is not something which existed in the crystal only in a less developed form. There is nothing at all like it in the crystal. . . . When from vegetable life we rise to animal life, here again we find something original and unique, — unique at least as compared with the animal. From animal life we ascend again to spiritual life. And here also is something new, something still more unique. He who lives the spiritual life has a distinct kind of life added to all the other phases of life which he manifests, — a kind of life infinitely more distinct than is the active life of a plant from the inertia of a stone. . . . The natural man belongs essentially to this present order of things. He is endowed simply with a higher quality of the natural animal life. But it is life of so poor a quality that it is not life at all. 'He that hath not the Son *hath not life;* but he that hath the Son hath life,' — a new and distinct and supernatural endowment. He is not of this world, he is of the timeless state of eternity. *It doth not yet appear what he shall be.*"

In the chapter on Classification this distinction is further elaborated, and a picture drawn of the merely moral or upright man, that leaves him very low down indeed in the scale of life, when contrasted with the Scotch Presbyterian. He is still a stone compared with the plant. " Here, for example, are two characters, pure and elevated, adorned with conspicuous virtues, stirred by lofty impulses, and commanding a spontaneous admiration from all who look upon them, — may not this similarity of outward form be accompanied by a total dissimilarity of inward nature?" And he adds that the difference is really as profound and basal as that between the organic and the inorganic.

As rhetoric or as theology, one need care little

for all this; but when it is uttered as science, as it is here, it is quite another matter. When it is declared that a man, say like Emerson, in comparison with the general of the Salvation Army, is a crystal compared to a flower, and the declaration is made in the name and with the authority of science, it is time to protest. In fact, to aver that the finest specimens of the race who lived before the advent of Christianity, or who have lived since, and honestly withheld their assent from the Calvinistic interpretation of it, came short of the higher life and the true destiny of man, as much as the stone comes short of the plant, may do as the personal opinion of a Scotch professor, but to announce such an opinion as the result of a scientific demonstration is an insult to science and an outrage upon human nature.

It is told that a celebrated wit once silenced an old Billingsgate fishwife by calling her a parallelogram. Professor Drummond calls the merely moral man a hexagon (see chapter on Classification), and there is just as much science in the one case as in the other. It is a mere calling of names, and the retort in both cases is likely to be, "You're another!" That there is a fundamental difference between the crystal and the cell we all know, but to call Plato or Marcus Aurelius a crystal, and Luther or Calvin a living organism, is purely gratuitous. To science Paul is no more alive than Plato. Both were master spirits, both made a deep and lasting impression upon the world, both are still living forces in the world of mind to-day. Theology may see a fundamental difference between the two, but science does not. Theology may attach its own meanings to the terms life and death, but science can attach but one meaning to them, — the meaning they have in the universal speech of mankind. Theology may say that "he that hath the Son hath life, and he that hath not the Son hath not life;" but is the statement any more scientific than it would be to say, "He that hath Confucius hath life, and he that hath not Confucius hath not life"? If Christ was the life in a biological and verifiable sense, then the proposition would carry its own proof. But the kind of life here referred to is a kind entirely unknown to science. The language, like the language of so much else in the New Testament, is the language of mysticism, and is not capable of verification by any process known to science. The facts that confirm it, if facts there are, lie entirely outside of the domain of scientific inquiry, direct or indirect.

As a matter of fact, and within the range of scientific demonstration, the difference beween the Christian and the non-Christian, between the moral and the orthodox citizen, in our day, is as little as the difference between Whig and Tory, or Republican and Democrat, — a difference of belief and of outward observance, and in no sense a fundamental

39

difference of life and character. Is it probable that a scientific commission could establish any essential differences, say between Professor Tyndall and Professor Drummond, any differences which the latter owed to his orthodoxy that enhanced his worth as a man, as a citizen, as a father, as a husband, or as a man of trust and responsibility, over and above the former? It would probably be found that both possessed "that inbred loyalty unto virtue" of Sir Thomas Browne which certainly is the main matter in this world, and more's the pity if it is not the main matter in the next.

Our professor's argument from analogy breaks down on nearly every page by his confounding the particular with the universal, and substituting the exceptional, the hypothetical, for the natural and provable. The error is the same as if Bishop Butler had sought to prove from the *general* course of nature, such as the changing of worms into flies, the hatching of eggs into birds, the passage of infancy into manhood, that some *particular* men were endowed with immortal souls and lived after the dissolution of the body. But the bishop made the two sides of his equation equal; he started with the universal and he ended with the universal, and claimed immortality for *all* men. Drummond, on the other hand, seeks to prove a particular and exceptional fact by its analogy to a general law of nature. In his chapter on Conformity to Type, the leading idea is that every kind of organism conforms to the type of that which begat it: the oak to the oak, the bird to the bird. An incontrovertible statement, certainly. Now, what is the analogy? This, namely, that all Christians conform to the Christ-type, and are not begotten by themselves, but by Christ. Where is the *force* of the analogy? One fails to see it, because the argument proceeds from the universal to the particular again; a principle which is true of all birds, and all oaks, is true of only some men. All men are not Christians. Moreover, Professor Drummond urges that they cannot all be Christians, and that the scheme of Christianity does not require or intend that they shall all be Christians.

To give the analogy force requires that the law be as general in the one case as in the other. Every bird is a bird unconditionally; it is born a bird and dies a bird, and can be nothing else but a bird; and to show the same universal law of conformity to type, working in both cases, every man must be a Christian on the same terms: it must be shown to be the law of his being from which there is no escape. If one man fails to become a Christian, the law is broken as truly as if a bird's egg were to hatch out a mouse, or an acorn to produce a cabbage. But in the scientific Calvinism of Professor Drummond, every bird is not a bird; only one here and there has the bird-form thrust upon it. The number of Christians is of necessity very limited. Salvation, and hence immortality, are for the few, not for the many. Our Christian philosopher is actually driven by the necessities of his argument into maintaining the truth of a special and limited immortality. Immortality is not for the whole human race, any more than the principle of life is for the whole inorganic kingdom.

" Some mineral, but not all, become vegetable; some vegetable, but not all, become animal; some animal, but not all, become human; some human, but not all, become divine." But the principle is the same as if all mineral did become vegetable, etc. It *may* become vegetable, probably in its turn will become vegetable; there is no partiality or preference on the part of Nature. The same in the higher spheres. All men are approximately divine, such men as Plato and Paul vastly more so, of course, than the great mass of men; but the difference is one of degree, not of kind, like the difference between the half flyers and the perfect flyers among the birds. Yet Professor Drummond dares affirm that certain members of a species are endowed with a *kind* of life which is denied to certain other members of the same species, and he makes this declaration, not in the name of theology, but in the name of science!

Far be it from me to seek to belittle or discredit the true Christian life of any man or woman, — the

life that conforms, however imperfectly, to the example set by Jesus of Nazareth.

What I urge is that the natural philosopher is
bound to consider such a life as not contingent upon
a certain belief, or the acceptance of certain dogmas,
or upon any one historical event, but that it has
been possible to man in all ages, and is more possible now than it was in the time of Socrates, only
by virtue of the force of the teachings and of the
immortal example of the founder of Christianity.

To the impartial observer, such a man as Julian
the Apostate appears as about the best Christian of
his time, although he utterly abjured Christianity,
and was a pagan to the last drop of his blood. To
be a Christian, in the higher sense, is to live a certain life, not to subscribe to a certain creed; or, in
the words of Milton (though Milton would probably
have repudiated this application of his words), it is
to "dare to think, to speak, and to be that which
the highest wisdom has in every age taught to be
best."

It may not be amiss for me to supplement or
qualify the foregoing pages with a page or two
which have a different bearing. In the first place,
let me say that I have not so much spoken for
myself therein as I have spoken for that attitude of
mind which makes science or exact knowledge possible, — a state of mind which in our time, I am

aware, is carrying things with a high hand. I know full well that science does not make up the sum total of life ; that there are many things in this world that count for more than exact knowledge. A noble sentiment, an heroic impulse, courage, and self-sacrifice, — how all your exact demonstrations pale before these things! But I recognize the fact that within its own sphere science is supreme, and its sphere is commensurate with human reason; and that, when an appeal is made to it, we must abide by the result. Theology assumes to be a science, the science of God, and as such the evidence, the proof upon which it relies, must stand the test of reason, or be capable of verification. Religion, as a sentiment, as an aspiration after the highest good, is one thing; but formulated into a system of theology and assuming to rest upon exact demonstrations, is quite another. As such, it is exposed to the terrible question, Is it true? In other words, it comes within the range of science, and must stand its fire. When miracles are brought forward as an evidence of the truth of Christianity, the natural philosopher is bound to ask, Do miracles take place?

If our life were alone made up of reason or of exact knowledge, science would be all in all to us. So far as it is made up of these things, science must be our guide. But probably four fifths of life is quite outside of the sphere of science; four fifths of life is sentiment. The great ages of the world have been ages of sentiment; the great literatures are the embodiments of sentiment. Patriotism is a sentiment; love, benevolence, admiration, worship, are all sentiments.

Man is a creature of emotions, of attractions, and of intuitions, as well as of reason and calculation. Science cannot deepen your love of country, or of home and family, or of honor or purity; nor enhance your enjoyment of a great poem or work of art, or of an heroic act, or of the beauty of nature; nor quicken your religious impulses. To know is less than to love ; to know the reason of things is less than to be quick to the call of duty. Unless we approach the Bible, or any of the sacred books of antiquity, or the great poems, or nature itself, — a bird, a flower, a tree, — in other than the scientific spirit, the spirit whose aim is to express all values in the terms of the reason or the understanding, we shall miss the greatest good they hold for us. We are not to approach them in a spirit hostile to science, but with a willingness to accept what science can give, but knowing full well that there is a joy in things and an insight into them which science can never give. There is probably nothing in the Sermon on the Mount that appeals to our scientific faculties, yet there are things here by reason of which the world is vastly the gainer. Indeed, nearly all the recorded utterances of Jesus rise into regions where science cannot follow. "Take no thought of the body." "He that would save his life shall lose it." "Except ye become as little children, ye cannot enter the kindom of heaven." These things are in almost flat contradiction of the precepts of science.

It may be noted that Jesus turned away from or rebuked the more exact, skeptical mind that asked for a sign, that wanted proof of everything, and that his appeal was to the more simple, credulous, and enthusiastic. He chose his disciples from among this class, men of faith and emotion, not too much given to reasoning about things. In keeping with this course of action, nearly all his teachings were by parables. In fact, Jesus was the highest type of the mystical, parable-loving, Oriental mind, as distinguished from the exact, science-loving, Occidental mind.

Let us not make the mistake of supposing that all truth is scientific truth, or that only those things are true and valuable which are capable of verification by the reason or by experience. Truth has many phases, and reaches us through many channels. There is a phase of truth which is apprehended by what we call taste, as poetic truth, literary truth; another phase which is felt by the conscience, as moral truth; and still another, which addresses the soul as the highest spiritual and religious truths. All these are subjective truths, and may be said to be qualities of the mind, but they are just as real for all that as the objective truths of science. These

latter are the result of a demonstration, but the
former are a revelation in the strict sense. Such
a poet as Wordsworth, such a writer as Emerson,
speaks to a certain order of minds. In each case
there is a truth which is colored by, or rather is
the product of, the man's idiosyncrasy. In science
we demand a perfectly colorless, transparent medium; the personality of the man must be kept out
of the work, but in poetry and in general literature
the personality of the man is the chief factor. The
same is true of the great religious teachers; they
give us themselves. They communicate to us, in a
measure, their own exalted spirituality. The Paul-
ine theology, or the theology which has been de-
duced from the teachings of Paul, may not be true
as a proposition in Euclid is true, but the sentiment which animated Paul, his religious fervor, his
heroic devotion to a worthy cause, were true, were
real, and this is stimulating and helpful. Shall we
make meat and drink of sacred things? Shall we
value the Bible only for its literal, outward truth?
Convince me that the historical part of the Bible is
not true, that it is a mere tissue of myths and superstitions, that none of those things fell out as there
recorded; and yet the vital, essential truth of the
Bible is untouched. Its morals, its ethics, its poetry, are forever true. Its cosmology may be entirely
unscientific, probably is so, but its power over the
human heart and soul remains. Indeed, the Bible

is the great deep of the religious sentiment, the primordial ocean. All other expressions of this sentiment are shallow and tame compared with the briny deep of the Hebrew Scriptures. What storms of conscience sweep over it; what upreaching, what mutterings of wrath, what tenderness and sublimity, what darkness and terror, are in this book! What pearls of wisdom it holds, what gems of poetry! Verily, the Spirit of the Eternal moves upon it. Whether, then, there be a personal God or not, whether our aspirations after immortality are well founded or not, yet the Bible is such an expression of the awe, and reverence, and yearning of the human soul in the presence of the facts of life and death, and of the power and mystery of the world, as pales all other expression of these things; not a cool, calculated expression of it, but an emotional, religious expression of it. To demonstrate its divergence from science is nothing; from the religious aspirations of the soul it does not diverge.

What I wish to say, therefore, is that we are conscious of emotions and promptings that are of deeper birth than the reason, that we are capable of a satisfaction in the universe quite apart from our exact knowledge of it, and that the religious sentiment of man belongs to this order of truths. This sentiment takes on various forms; the forms themselves are not true, but the sentiment is. To recur to my former illustration of the constellations, —

however fantastic the figures which the soul has pictured upon the fathomless dome, the stars *are* there; the religious impulse remains.

It is perhaps inevitable that systems should arise, that creeds should be formed, and that the name of science should be invoked in their behalf, but the wise man knows they are perishable, and that the instinct that gave them birth alone endures. What is the value of this instinct? It would be presumption for me to attempt to estimate it, or to hope to disclose its full significance. Its history is written in the various ethnic religions, often written in revolting forms and observances. But it tends more and more to purify itself, rises more and more toward the conception of the fact that the kingdom of heaven is within and not without ; and this purification has in our day unquestionably been forwarded by what we call science.

IV

NATURAL VERSUS SUPERNATURAL

OUR theological professors make a mistake when they think they have weakened or parried the objections of science to their doctrines by pointing to the fact that science is constantly revising or reversing its own conclusions ; that what was deemed good science at one time is found to be false science at another. " This modern infallibility which men call science " is a phrase used by a modern doctor of divinity in criticising a recent paper of my own on Science and Theology.

" We who are yet upon the safe side of the ministerial dead-line," he says, " can remember when it was scientific to assert the diverse origin of the race ' from four or six pairs ' of progenitors ; and we have come to the day in which science will not leave us as much as Adam and Eve for a beginning. We have learned the igneous origin of granite, just in time to be commanded to unlearn it, and substitute an aqueous origin." And the conclusion, therefore, is that science is discredited, and that he who builds upon it plants his house upon the sands. But science makes no claim to infallibility ; it leaves that claim to be made by theology. "This shifting of positions and this changing of results" but marks its growth, its development ; and it is precisely this active and inquiring spirit, this readiness to correct its errors, and this eagerness to reach a larger generalization, that makes it the enemy of the traditional theology. It abandoned the Ptolemaic system of astronomy for the Copernican, because the latter was found to be the most complete generalization ; but theology still adheres to its Ptolemaic system of things. To seek to discredit science because it has made mistakes, and has had to unlearn many things, is to deny the very principle of progress ; it is to reflect upon the child because he grows into a man. The main outlines of the physical universe science has undoubtedly finally settled ; the great facts of astronomy and geology are not to be reversed or set aside. It is only in the details, the filling in of the picture, that errors are still likely to occur. No, what theology has to fear, and what is working such mischief with it, is not the " infallibility " of science, but it is the scientific spirit, the spirit that demands complete verification, that applies past experience to new problems, that sees that immutable laws lie at the bottom of all phenomena, and that is skeptical of all exceptions to the logical course of events until they are irrefragably proved.

Science is ignorant enough, without doubt, about many things. After it has done its best, the mys-

Slabsides, Mr. Burroughs' Study

tery of creation is as deep as before. But what it has taught the race, and what the race can never unlearn, is that the sequence of cause and effect is inviolable, that the order of the physical universe is rational, that creation is not an historical event but a perpetual process, that there is no failure and no disorder in nature, and that to approximate to anything like a right understanding of things the personal, or the *anthropocentric*, point of view must be abandoned.

Our doctor of divinity is unfortunate in confronting the kind of " exceptions " which I aver science cannot recognize with the fact that water, in opposition to all other material substances, *expands* under a certain degree of cold. But is there any known exception to this law of water? Has water ever been known to reverse this process in freezing? If so, the exception would indeed stagger science; it would be a miracle. A child born of a woman, but without an earthly father, and of a superhuman species, is the kind of exception which I averred science cannot recognize; but does this bear any analogy to the exceptional behavior of water while freezing, when compared with other substances? It used to be believed that in every animal that possessed a circulation the blood always took one definite and invariable direction, but in 1824, Huxley says, it was discovered that a class of animals called *Ascidians* furnished an exception; the heart of these animals, after beating a certain number of times, stops, and then begins to beat in the opposite way, so as to reverse the course of the blood, which returns by and by to its original direction. Such an exception does not disturb the man of science; it only teaches him greater caution in making his deductions. But if one Ascidian, and but *one*, could be found whose heart beat like that of other animals, that would be a puzzle to him. Or if one comet, and only one, should appear carrying its tail toward the sun instead of from it, cometary astronomy would be reduced to chaos. A floating feather is no exception to the law of gravitation, but a floating stone and a falling feather would be an exception. Science as well as experience finds exceptions to general rules everywhere, but these exceptions are constant and as strictly the result of natural law as anything else. Faith in the continuity of nature, upon which the scientist builds, no less than every man in the conduct of his life, does not mean sameness or identity of all physical processes, but it means identity of these processes under like conditions. Given the same conditions, and the same results *always* follow. Water obeys its laws under low temperature, and iron its. It is not long since that the Bishop of Carlisle urged as an argument against the uniformity of nature the fact that the weather is changeable! If his lordship could have shown that the laws which govern the formation of clouds and the precipitation of rain and snow are changeable, or ever work inversely, he would have made out his case. The fathers of the church believed that the flesh of the peacock never decayed. St. Augustine said he had ascertained by experiment that this is a fact. If this were so, it would indeed be a remarkable exception; but the man of science would at once set about ascertaining its natural cause, without for one moment attributing it to a supernatural one. But without trying the experiment ourselves, does any sane man to-day doubt that either the saint deceived himself, or else that he was not honest? His statement is incredible because it contradicts all the rest of our knowledge relating to the decomposition of animal tissue.

I suppose the last thing our fathers would have thought of doing would have been to try to reconcile their conception of Christianity with their stores of natural knowledge. They did not feel the need, which we to-day feel so keenly, of any such reconciliation. They cherished their faith as something apart, something not founded in the order of this world, something to which science and all that pertains to the " natural man " are necessarily strangers. The order of this world is carnal; it is full of evil, and is separated by an impassable gulf from the sacred and the divine. A vast number of most excellent and pious people still feel in this way about their religious belief; it is all the more sacred and pre-

true that half-formed, half-developed minds, which means the great mass of the people of any age, rather draw back from exposing their faith to a light so common, so secular as that of reason. Plutarch quotes Sophocles as saying that the Deity is

" Easy to wise men, who can truth discern,"

but adds that the vulgar look with high veneration upon whatever is extravagant and extraordinary, and conceive a more than common sanctity to lie concealed under the veil of obscurity. The average mind clings to the mysterious, the supernatural. Goethe, as lately quoted by Matthew Arnold, said those who have science and art have religion ; and added, let those who have not science and art have religion, that is, let them have the popular faith ; let them have this escape, because the others are closed to them. Without any hold upon the ideal, or any insight into the beauty and fitness of things, the people turn from the tedium and the grossness and prosiness of daily life, to look for the divine, the sacred, the saving, in the wonderful, the miraculous, and in that which baffles reason. The disciples of Jesus thought of the kingdom of heaven as some external condition of splendor and pomp and power which was to be ushered in by hosts of trumpeting angels, and the Son of man in great glory, riding upon the clouds, and not for one moment as the still small voice within them. To find the divine and the helpful in the mean and familiar, to find religion without the aid of any supernatural machinery, to see the spiritual, the eternal life in and through the life that now is — in short, to see the rude, prosy earth as a star in the heavens, like the rest, is indeed the lesson of all others the hardest to learn.

But we must learn it sooner or later. There surely comes a time when the mind perceives that this world is the work of God also and not of devils, and that in the order of nature we may behold the ways of the Eternal; in fact, that God is here and now in the humblest and most familiar fact, as sleepless and active as ever he was in old Judea. This perception has come and is coming to more minds to-day than ever before: this perception of the modernness of God, of the modernness of inspiration, of the modernness of religion ; that there was never any more revelation than there is now, never any more miracles or signs and wonders, never any more conversing of God with man, never any more Garden of Eden, or fall of Adam, or thunder of Sinai, or ministering angels, than there is now ; in fact, that these things are not historical events, but inward experiences and perceptions perpetually renewed or typified in the growth of the race. This is the modern gospel ; this is the one vital and formative religious thought of modern times.

The mind that has fully opened to this perception no longer divorces its faith from its reason, no longer rests in the idea of a dualism in creation, or of opposition between God and the world, and cannot feel at ease until its religious belief is in harmony with its natural knowledge. The two must not be at war. What we hope for, what we aspire to, must be consistent with what we know. Faith and science must, indeed, go hand in hand. The conception of religion as a miraculous scheme for man's redemption interpolated into history, God's original design with reference to man having miscarried, is entirely undermined and overthrown by the perception of the unity and consistency of creation as revealed by science.

Who does not see that it adds vastly to the credibility of a doctrine or theory to find that it fits in with other things, that it is not an exception or an isolated circumstance, but is in a line with facts and principles of the truth of which we are already assured? Suppose the theory of Christianity, as popularly held, had something like the breadth of application, or the same warrant and basis in the constitution of things as has, say, the theory of evolution or the doctrine of the conservation of energy; or suppose the dogma of vicarious atonement pleased the mind and harmonized with our sense of the fitness of creation like the modern doctrine of embryology, namely, that embryology is a repetition of past history, that every animal in its development from

the egg assumes successively, though briefly, all the
forms through which its ancestors have come in the
course of the long stretch of geological ages, should
we not all unhesitatingly accept it as true? Would
there ever have been any doubters and skeptics? I
think not. It is because these things have no such
warrant and basis, no such agreement with our
perception of the order of the world, that doubters
and skeptics exist ; it is because they break completely with all the rest of our knowledge of creation.

There is a very marked activity in the theological mind to-day which has for its end the bridging
over of the gulf which exists between natural and
what is called " revealed " truth. Half a dozen recent works might be named of which this is the
principal aim. That eloquent preacher Frederick
W. Robertson sought in one of his sermons to give
a natural basis to the dogma of vicarious sacrifice,
perhaps the most incredible dogma in the popular
creed. See, says the eloquent divine, how the mineral must decay before the vegetable can grow; how
the vegetable must die before the animal can live ;
how the animal must perish before we can have
roast beef for our dinner. The dove is stricken
down by the hawk, the deer by the lion, the winged
fish falls into the jaws of the dolphin. " It is the
solemn law of vicarious sacrifice again ; " and so
still higher. " The anguish of the mother is the

condition of the child's life." Every civilization is founded upon the labors and sufferings of those who went before. When this law of self-sacrifice is consciously obeyed it becomes the highest moral virtue and reaches heroism. Now, all this is true ; it is a part of our natural knowledge. But it is not vicarious sacrifice ; it is not sacrifice at all in the true sense. It is the order of the succession of life in nature. The living present is always reared upon the dead past. Not only men, but races and nations,

> "May rise on stepping-stones
> Of their dead selves to higher things."

The six noble citizens of Calais who surrendered themselves to the vengeance of the English king were offering themselves as a vicarious sacrifice. They were willing to die, that their fellows might live ; but this act bears no resemblance to the order of nature above alluded to, and from which the great preacher drew his illustration. It rises to a region of which unconscious nature knows nothing — the region of heroism. But neither fact nor set of facts contains any hint that can lead to a rational explanation of how the death of Christ benefited mankind other than in the way the death of every hero benefits us. This is an esoteric, mysterious doctrine upon which no light can be thrown by an appeal to any known fact or law of the visible universe.

The eloquent preacher tries to help out his analogy by an original conception of Sin as "a single world spirit, exactly as electricity, with which the universe is charged, is indivisible, imponderable, one, so that you cannot separate it from the great ocean of fluid. The electric spark that slumbers in the dewdrop is part of the flood which struck the oak. Had that spark not been there, it could be demonstrated that the whole previous constitution of the universe might have been different and the oak not have been struck." Every separate act of sin is the manifestation of an original principle as broad and universal as this — the world spirit, the spirit of evil. Grant this, and still the connection cannot be made. Grant that this world spirit slew all the prophets, opposes the good in every age, and crucified "the Just One" himself, as, of course, it did and does, how did the death of Christ modify or conquer or remove this spirit, or shield man from the supposed wrath of his Creator, in any other way than the death of every just person for a worthy cause accomplishes these ends? These are mysteries that cannot be explained, or the explanation even hinted at. The human faculties of reason and insight can never fathom them. Dying that others may live is truly the order of this universe, its natural order. But what examples history affords of its having been in so many instances the conscious human order — the order which makes heroes! Even in our selfish and materialistic age, as it is called, not a year passes but our pulse is quickened by the recital of some act of heroism during disaster upon the sea or in the mines or in burning cities, wherein men have calmly faced death that others might have a chance to live. But there is no analogy here to the popular theory of the sufferings and death of Christ. All men have to suffer the pangs of mortality just the same, and the consequences of sin just the same. When our theologians say that "Christ suffered for our sins, and that, because he suffered, our sins are forgiven," they make a statement that cannot be rationally conceived ; they use a language not comprehensible by human sense — the language of mysticism.

When we regard sin disinterestedly and in the light of our real knowledge, we find it but a relative term. It is not a positive thing as electricity is, but the absence of a thing, as cold is the absence of heat, or as darkness is the absence of light. It is the imperfection of human nature when tried by its highest possibilities. The theological conception of sin as imputed guilt has no more place in rational knowledge than sorcery has. The deeper our insight into the method of nature, or the more we are impressed with the order and consistency of the world, the more incredible the popular Christianity seems to us. To the man of science the old theology is like the traditional conception of angels — men with both wings and arms.

63

This conception breaks with the structural plan of all vertebrates just as theology does with the law of cause and effect. Human beings with wings in place of arms, might be contrary to the fact ; but such a conception does not violate the homologies of nature, but beings with both wings and arms have no counterpart in the world. They are not merely contrary to experience, they are contrary to the fundamental principle of structure that runs through the animal kingdom. But when these armed and winged beings were first conceived of, this fact was not known as it is now, and the *un*-natural element in Christianity could not have been appreciated in past ages as it is to-day.

The doctrinal part of the popular Christianity, its supernaturalism, is an inheritance from the past as much as witchcraft or magic is. But it did not break with human knowledge then ; it was in strict keeping with the elements of the marvelous and the exceptional, of which human knowledge was so largely made up. There was no science in those days, no conception of the course of human or natural events as the result of immutable law. The personal point of view prevailed in everything. Everything revolved about man ; superhuman beings took sides for or against him. Indeed, so far as science or a rational conception of things is concerned, the fathers of the church, and the framers of our popular theology, were mere children. Considerations were all-powerful with them which to-day would not have a feather's weight with a man of ordinary intelligence. Children readily, even eagerly, believe almost any impossible thing you may tell them about nature. As yet they have no insight into the course of nature, or of the law of cause and effect, no fund of experience to serve as a touchstone to the false or the impossible. The same was true of the fathers, and of the races that witnessed the advent of Christianity, — great in moral and spiritual matters, but mere children so far as the development of their scientific faculties were concerned ; and it is from the scientific faculties that theology, as such, proceeds. Theology is an attempt to define to the understanding the basis of man's religious convictions and aspirations ; it aims to be the science of God's dealings with man and nature, and as such it is bound to share the infirmity of the logical and scientific faculty of the times in which it arises.

The contemporaries of Jesus thought it not unreasonable that John the Baptist should come to life after his head had been taken off; that the prophet Elias should reappear upon earth, or that Jeremiah should come back. These notions were in strict keeping with the belief in the marvelous and the supernatural that then possessed men's minds. The four Gospels were a growth out of this atmosphere, and the current theology is a continuation of the same faith in prodigies as opposed to natural occurrences. The fathers knew little more about the true order of the physical universe than savages. They believed, for instance, the use of the spade made the earth fertile because it was of the form of a cross; that the sun, moon, and stars shone less brightly since the fall. Irenæus gave, as his reasons for accepting the four Gospels and no more, the fact that there are four universal winds and four quarters of the earth, and because living creatures are quadriform. Origen believed that the sun, moon, and stars were living, rational beings, capable of sinning and subject to vanity, and that they prayed to the Supreme Being through his only-begotten Son. Tertullian shared the belief of his contemporaries that the hyena changes its sex every year, being alternately male and female. Clement of Rome believed the story of the phœnix, that wonderful bird of Arabia, which was said to live five hundred years; and when it died at the end of that time, that a worm sprang from its decaying flesh which soon became a new phœnix, which forthwith took up the bones of its defunct parent and flew away to the city of Heliopolis, in Egypt, and laid them on the altar of the sun. The natural philosopher has always taught that " death is a law and not a punishment," but " the fathers taught it is a penal infliction introduced into the world on account of the sin of Adam, which was also the cause of the appearance of all noxious plants, of all convulsions in the material globe, and, as was sometimes asserted, even of a diminution of the light of the sun." How dormant and puerile man's scientific faculties were during the early centuries of Christianity, when the foundations of the science of theology were laid, is well illustrated in a work called the " Christian Opinion concerning the World," by the monk Cosmas, of the sixth century. Cosmas taught that the earth was literally a tabernacle, because St. Paul speaks of it as such, and that Moses exactly copied its form in his tabernacle. It is a flat parallelogram, twice as long as it is broad, roofed in by the sky, which is *glued* to the outer edges of the earth. It consists of two stories, in one of which dwell the blessed, and in the other the angels. It is from the type of mind that conceived such notions of the universe as this that we inherit our theology. But it may be replied, men may be feeble in science but great in religion. True, the fathers, many of them, were great in religion, they were great on the moral and spiritual side; but the system of theology they founded aims to be a science; it deals with exact propositions; it is not the work of their subjective religious natures but of their scientific faculties, and as such it is just as artificial, just as puerile and unreal, as the notions of the physical universe to which I have adverted.

The whole Christian dispensation, as expounded

by the popular theology, is as little in keeping with the physical order of the world as disclosed by science, or with the natural moral order as disclosed by the conscience, as Indian medicine is in keeping with modern therapeutics. The whole scheme hinges upon the fall of Adam in paradise as an historical event, an act of disobedience on the part of the original progenitor of the human family, in consequence of which sin and death entered the world, and the suffering and death of Jesus became necessary to bring about a reconciliation between an angry God and rebellious man; with the attendant doctrine of the mystery of the atonement, of salvation by grace, of the eternal punishment of the pre-Christian nations, etc. Now this conception as science, or as a rational explanation of the world as it is, and of man's salvation, is on a par with Cosmas's theory of the earth with the sky glued to the outer edges. It shows the working of the same type of mind, it rests upon the same arbitrary and artificial view of things.

But in all these matters the question now is whether the ancient or the modern point of view shall prevail; whether evolution or revelation is the law of the world. The ancient point of view, as we have seen, was exclusive and arbitrary; it looked upon the universe as something *made* and governed by a being or beings external to it. In medicine it regarded all disease as the work of evil spirits, that were to be exorcised by charms or amulets or incantations. In politics it inculcated the divine right of kings, that the king can do no wrong. In political economy it taught that the interests of nations were mutually antagonistic and destructive of one another. In physical science it encouraged the notions we have seen. The fathers taught that all men were under condemnation from the moment of their birth, and that at death the souls of unbaptized infants went straight to hell. St. Augustine taught, and the Catholic church still holds, that when water from the hands of a priest falls upon the head of an unconscious infant, a miraculous change is wrought in its spiritual nature, — a change by which it becomes essentially a new and a higher being; and the church says, with characteristic charity, of him who believes not this impossible doctrine, "Let him be accursed!"

It is this type of mind which fostered alchemy, astrology, sorcery, witchcraft, and demonology. The air and the earth and the waters swarmed with spirits, good and evil; disease, pestilence, storms, fires, and floods were the work of evil spirits; the more kindly motions of nature were the work of good spirits. A decrepit old woman could turn herself into a wolf and devour her neighbor's flocks. Meteors, eclipses, and comets were portents sent directly from heaven for the warning of mankind.

How has all this been changed! How completely

the mind of man now faces the other way, in everything except in theology — faces toward a natural
explanation of all phenomena!

Let no hasty reader conclude that I am arguing
against the reality of religion; I am only arguing
against the reality of magic and miracles; against
the conception of Christianity as a scheme for man's
salvation *interpolated* into human history, and in
no sense one with the constitution of the world;
against the idea that the spiritual life is in no sense
a possible development of man's natural capabilities,
but something superadded from without, — a unique
and peculiar kind of life, which was made possible
to man by the life and death of Christ, and in no
way possible before that event. It is not an evolution from man's proper nature; it comes from the
opposite direction, and is external and supplemen-
tary. "Christianity," say the Andover doctors,
"is a source of knowledge concerning God which is
not given by the external universe nor by the constitution of man, but only by Christ." Religion is
still conceived of as a miraculous scheme to remedy
some miscarriage or failure in the plan of God's dealings with man, a failure whereby his relation to the
race was radically changed. It is looked upon as
something naturally foreign to man, something to be
ingrafted upon him from without, not related at all
to his natural capacity for virtue and goodness;
something which a blameless man may live and die

without, but which a cut-throat during the last moments of his life upon the scaffold may, by what
is called an act of faith and repentance, obtain!
Against such notions I am directing my argument; I
am urging that the sentiment of religion is the same
in all ages and lands, differing in its outward forms,
but not in its inward essence, just as the sentiment of patriotism or of loyalty is the same. How
is a reasonable man to favor any scheme that rules
out the religion of Plato and Zeno and Seneca and
Epictetus and Cicero and Lucretius, or of Spinoza
or of Darwin, as of no avail, as only snares of Satan?
The flowering of man's spiritual nature is as natural
and as strict a process of evolution as the opening
of a rose or a morning-glory. The vital inflorescent
forces are from within, and are continuous from the
root up. But there is this difference: While the
plant must have a congenial environment, light,
warmth, etc., the human flowering often takes place
amid the most adverse surroundings, but no more so
in the religious sphere than in the intellectual.

Neither would I say that the " conversion " upon
which our Puritan ancestors laid such stress, and
which is so dramatically illustrated in the case of
Paul, was not genuine. It was genuine to them, but
it was entirely a subjective phenomenon, like the
faith cures we now often hear about; it was the
power of the imagination working upon the conscience. It is not a necessary or universal experi-

ence, even among religious people. It may be said without any irreverence that it has gone out of fashion. The predisposition for that kind of experience no longer exists. "The belief in witchcraft," says Milman, " made people fancy themselves witches," and the belief in the efficacy of sudden conversions led to these kinds of moral and spiritual earthquakes.

Science looks upon religion as belonging to the sphere of the natural; it is the legitimate outcome of man's moral nature; the term that best expresses the complete development and flowering of all his faculties. To define it in the guarded terms which Principal Tulloch uses, namely, as " an inner power of divine mystery awakening the conscience," is to make it something external to man and more or less arbitrary and theological. This view the world has long clung to, but it must go — is going. The biblical writers had no theology; the Bible is strictly a religious book, and in no sense a theological treatise. Paul developed or outlined some theological notions; but wherein was Paul great — in his theology, or in his religious fervor; in his notions of predestination, or in his aspirations after righteousness? Jesus is as free from any theological bias as a child is from metaphysics. He taught but one thing; namely, that the kingdom of heaven is in the condition of the heart, a condition illustrated by his own life. The vast and elaborate system of theology which grew up out of his parables and his Orientalism, and overshadowed the world for fifteen hundred years or more, and begat some of the darkest crimes the history of man has to show, is as far from his spirit and that of his disciples as the east is from the west.

Undoubtedly, religion knows certain things in a more intimate and personal way than science does; so does poetry, so does literature; and science can understand how this is so. What we receive through the emotions is more vital and personal to us than what reaches us through the reason. The person in whose mind has been awakened a deep love of Jesus, comes to know Jesus in a way the mere outside observer does not; his spirit takes hold of the Christ idea, and is filled and modified by it to an extent the other is not. An emotional process is more potent than a rational process. The knowledge thus gained is no more truly knowledge, but it is more vital knowledge. It is not merely conviction; it is attraction and affiliation as well. But this is true not of Jesus merely; it is true of the whole range of our experience. If the flower or the bird or the tree awaken no emotion in the observer, will he ever come truly to know it? Unless we love an author, can we ever get at his deepest and most precious meaning? Hence Goethe said, "We learn to know nothing but what we love." In this light, science sees that the love of Jesus, or of God, may transform a man's life, not by any peculiar and supernatural process, but by a universal and well-known law; namely, that we grow like that which we love. Every object we look upon or think of with the emotion of love, that object in a measure we become. But to begin with, we are not capable of loving it until we are in some degree, either potentially or actually, like it. No radically un-Christ-like nature will ever come to love Jesus. Hence the subtile truth in the old doctrines that have been so hardly and literally stated, "Except God work in you to will and to do," etc. The Christian, the virtuous, pious soul, is born and not made, just as truly as is the poet or the artist, and the "new birth" in the one case can mean no more that it does in the other. The true Christian only gives a new name to his natural piety or aptitude for Christianity, but in no sense is there a radical change of nature. It is simply a transference of allegiance, as in the case of Paul. All these things may be so stated as to harmonize with the rest of our knowledge, but as expounded in theological books they do not so harmonize, but run counter to it completely. Subjective truths are stated as if they were objective *facts;* qualities of the mind and spirit are expounded as if they were realities of the experience.

Certain of the alleged miracles of the New Testament, as the healing of the sick by an act of faith, agree with what we now know to be true. Certain human ailments, mainly diseases of the mind and the nervous system, have in recent times undoubtedly yielded to an act of faith in the supreme efficacy of certain rites, or to an unwonted mental resolution. But the remedy is subjective and not objective. The virtue was not in the hem of the garment touched, but in the effort of the will of the person who touched it.

The things that are at variance with the rest of our knowledge in the New Testament are such as grew up naturally in a superstitious age around the person and teachings of such a transcendent being as Jesus was, — the notion that he was more than human, that he had no earthly father, that he had some superhuman control over the forces of nature, that he rose from the dead, that his death bore some mysterious relation to the sins of the world. When a man talks about the value and importance of the ethics of Christianity, — of charity, of mercy, of justice, of gentleness, of purity, of righteousness, or of what the world has in all ages taught to be highest and best, — we can understand him; he speaks the language of truth and soberness. When he says with Marcus Aurelius, that there is but one thing of real value, "to cultivate truth and justice, and live without anger in the midst of lying and unjust men;" or when he says with Peregrinus, that "the wise man will not sin, though both gods and men should overlook the deed, for it is not through the fear of punishment or of shame that he abstains from sin: it is from the desire and obligation of what is just and good;" or when he says with Micah, "And what doth the Lord require of thee but to do justly and to love mercy, and to walk humbly with thy God?" or when he says with Solomon that "the fear of the Lord is to hate evil;" or with Jeremiah, "He judged the cause of the poor and needy — was not this to know me? saith the Lord;" or when he says with St. James, "Pure religion and undefiled before God and the Father is this, to visit the fatherless and widows in their affliction, and to keep himself unspotted from the world," he gives utterance to sentiments that appeal to the best there is in every man, and that agree with the highest wisdom of all ages and races. Science can understand it and verify it.

But when he talks to us about Jesus in the language of the evangelical churches, — about the atonement, original sin, santification, and saving grace, — he simply uses a jargon that may mean something to him, but can mean nothing at all to an outsider. He states things as facts which have no ground either in reason or experience; they belong to a world apart, which neither the rest of our knowledge nor our natural faculties of reason and observation can put us in communication with. He might just as well talk about the elixir of life or of the philosopher's stone. The traditional theology has undoubtedly proved itself a good working hypothesis with crude and half-developed minds, but upon what thoughtful and cultivated person does it now make an impression? No race has been lifted out of barbarism without the aid of supernatural machinery. Once lifted out, how prone we are to discredit the machinery! We have no further use for it. We have outgrown it. But the mass of mankind are slow to outgrow it. To the mass of mankind the miraculous element of Christianity still seems vital and of first importance. Discredit that, and you have discredited religion itself in their eyes. But not so with the philosopher, or with the man who is bent on seeing and knowing things exactly as they are.

I think it is in accordance with the rest of our knowledge that Christianity could not have made its way in the world, its superior ethical and moral system could not have gained the ascendency, without the cloud of myths in which it came enveloped. What a seal of authentication is put upon it by the myth of the resurrection of Jesus! How this fact stuns and overwhelms the ordinary mind! Was it Talleyrand who replied to some enthusiast who proposed to start a new religion, that he advised him to begin by getting himself crucified and to rise again on the third day? As a new cult founded upon reason alone, or as a natural religion alone, Christianity could not have coped with the supernatural religions that then possessed the world. Men's

77

minds were not prepared for it, and it is probably equally true that the mass of mankind are not yet prepared for a religion based upon natural knowledge alone. But the time is surely coming, and natural science is to be the chief instrument in bringing it about. The religious sense of man is less and less dependent upon thaumaturgical aids. It is beginning to hear God in the still small voice ; not in the tempest, nor in the earthquake, nor in the fire ; not in the marvelous, the extraordinary, the irrational, but in the quiet and familiar facts of nature and of life. The vulgar mind asks for a sign, a wonder ; but science has no sign, no wonder to show. It points to the simplest fact. Its relation toward the old theology is like that of Elisha toward Naaman. When Naaman came to the prophet to be cured of his leprosy, he expected Elisha to do some wonderful thing, some miracle. "Behold, I thought, He will surely come out to me, and stand, and call on the name of the Lord his God, and strike his hand over the place, and recover the leper." Instead of which the prophet simply told him to go and wash seven times in the Jordan and be clean. "My father," said his servant to the indignant Naaman, "if the prophet had bid thee do some great thing, wouldest thou not have done it? how much rather, then, when he saith to thee, Wash, and be clean ? "

The leprosy of the miraculous which taints men's

minds is to be got rid of in the same way: wash and be clean in the current of the sweet-flowing nature that is always near at hand, and that is always and everywhere the same.

Credulity is quite a different thing. Credulity may be defined as belief without proof in matters where proof is demanded and is within reach. Faith is belief without proof in matters where proof is impossible. Mankind have always been very credulous ; credulity is easy ; we all have to fight against it. But faith, as Dr. Fisher insists, is not easy ; it requires a strong effort of the will. Children are very credulous ; they believe whatever we tell them without proof. Indeed, they do not yet know what proof is. So with savage tribes, though with them credulity mainly runs into superstition. Credulity is the basis of superstition. When the mysterious, the preternatural, is brought into matters within reach of investigation, and the event or occurrence is referred to anti-mundane agencies, as in the case of haunted houses, that is one form of superstition.

When Professor Bryce was about to ascend Mount Ararat, he was told by the people at its base that the ascent was impossible ; that no human being would be permitted to behold the top of the sacred mountain. For all that, the plucky traveler thought he would put the matter to the test. He procured guides and set out. His guides failed him long before the summit was reached, but he pushed on alone, and scaled the peak. When he returned and had an interview with one of the religious dignitaries in the village near by, and his guide told the priest that the Englishman had been to the top of

Ararat, the priest smiled loftily and said it was impossible — no man had ever been to the top of the mountain. Here we have a case of credulity running into superstition, belief in the interference of the supernatural where proof or disproof was easy.

I lately read in the autobiography of the Italian sculptor, Dupré, an incident which affords a similar illustration. Dupré was an excellent man and a great artist, but he was not above superstition, as few of us are. He was driving one day down a steep, rugged mountain road, accompanied by his wife, when he distinctly heard the words, " *Stop, stop!* " As he continued, the words were repeated, and so impressed both himself and wife that he did stop and look about him, and called out to his supposed challenger. Seeing and hearing nothing more, he drove on, when " *Stop, stop, stop!* " again rang out from some place near them. Then he again stopped, and, much impressed and even alarmed, he and his wife both got out of the carriage, when he discovered that the linchpin that held one of the hind wheels was gone, and that the wheel was far bent over and just ready to drop off, and thus endanger the lives of the occupants. The pious artist was deeply impressed, and evidently regarded the warning voice as providential. But a little investigation would doubtless have dispelled the delusion. Probably if he had started up his horses after he and his wife left the carriage, he would have disto differ, that saved him in that case. Had the story had any element of the mysterious or preternatural in it, so as to have touched Johnson's religious fears and prejudices, he would doubtless have accepted it at once.

It was once commonly believed that the salamander could withstand fire, but an old Catholic traveler in the sixteenth century says he caught one and put it into the fire, and it died. But he believed the story of the basilisk; namely, that its look was fatal. He said, though, that it was necessary for the animal to look its victim in the eye at a certain distance. He saw a basilisk, but it was dead. If it had been living, probably he would not have been as ready to test its powers as he was those of the salamander. Like Dr. Johnson, he was not credulous unless his credulity could take a superstitious turn.

A good instance of the credulity of science in its youth is furnished by Albert Magnus, who in his book upon animals, in the sixteenth century, says that eels leave the water in the night, invade fields and gardens, and feed upon peas and lentils. A French missionary, writing on natural history in the seventeenth century, says of the humming bird that it passes the winter in a torpid state, hanging by its feet from the under side of a limb in the woods. The credulity of country people in reference to the divining-rod, or the efficacy of twigs of the beech or the willow in the hands of certain persons in locating hidden springs or water-veins, is equally childish.

Credulity and superstition have to do mainly with the visible material universe; faith with the spiritual, invisible world.

Faith is, as Amiel says in his "Journal," "certitude without proof," and is therefore opposed to science, which goes entirely upon proof. It is a moral rather than an intellectual certitude; a conviction of the heart — to use the old phraseology — rather than a persuasion of the mind. That is, it is arrived at through an emotional process, rather than through a logical one. In an over-intellectual and over-reflective age like ours, faith undoubtedly suffers a decline. It thrives best in stirring uncritical times. The scientific spirit is as inimical to it as frost to vegetation. In all the centuries of our era, except the present, reason has been the willing servant of faith. Faith has said to it, Go here, go there; prove this, prove that; and reason has obeyed with alacrity. In our day reason turns upon faith and questions its right to rule and to lead, and the result is an almost ruinous shrinkage of the old theological values.

Dr. Fisher insists upon the proofs of faith, but he fails to point them out. They are not to be apprehended by the rational faculties. They are subjective; they are in the heart and conscience of the individual, and cannot be communicated as proof. That there is a power not ourselves, a power in which we live, and move, and have our being, and of which all things are the garment and expression, is not a matter of faith, but of reason and sense. That this power is a personal being, the moral governor and ruler of the universe, as the old theology has it, or the loving father and protector, as the new teaches, is a matter of faith. We speak of the creed of the church as a system of faith. The acceptance of most of its tenets is an act of faith rather than of reason. That Jesus of Nazareth was born of a woman is a matter of reason; that he was born of a virgin and had no earthly father is a matter of faith. That he was persecuted, that he suffered and died upon the cross, we have no difficulty in believing; but that he rose from the dead, and ascended bodily up into heaven, is again a dogma that belongs solely to faith. And so with the rest of the Apostles' Creed.

There is a passage in Goethe's autobiography that bears upon this subject, and a very suggestive one.

"General, natural religion," he says, "properly speaking, requires no faith; for the persuasion that a great producing, regulating, and conducting Being conceals himself, as it were, behind nature, to make himself comprehensible to us, — such a conviction forces itself upon every one. Nay, if we for a moment let drop this thread which conducts us through life, it may be immediately and everywhere resumed. But it is different with a special religion which announces to us that this Great Being distinctly and preëminently interests himself for one individual, one family, one people, one country. This religion is founded on faith, which must be immovable if it would not be instantly destroyed. Every doubt of such a religion is fatal to it. One may return to conviction, but not to faith."

St. Paul saw the difficulties in the way of an appeal to reason, and said boldly that " no man can say that Jesus is the Lord but by the Holy Ghost." To expect a man to affirm it by his unaided reason, or upon any grounds of evidence that can be had, is to expect the impossible. But Dr. Fisher says we have proof in its nature experimental, like the verification of the calculations of the astronomer by an eclipse occurring exactly on time; namely, in the miracles. But if an appeal is made to reason, does he not see that reason demands proof that the miracles occurred? Eclipses take place in our day, but miracles do not. The laws and processes of nature are continuous, but theology introduces us to a world devoid of continuity.

Theologians lay much stress upon contemporary belief and opinion, — upon the statement of those who themselves either witnessed the miracles or simply voiced the popular belief in their reality.

as the death of Cæsar, for instance, which everybody believes in. Do we want any proof of the
death of Cæsar? Do not all men die? The manner
of his death would be the only question, and we do
not want very strong proof upon that point, since
thousands of other men have fallen by the knife
of the assassin. But in the alleged resurrection
of Jesus of Nazareth we have an event the like of
which never happened before or since, an event
that contradicts the whole experience of the human
race, an event which by its startling and unheard-of
character overwhelms the mind, and we are asked to
believe it as readily as we do the death of Cæsar, on
the authority of a book or books of uncertain date
and uncertain authorship, written by persons who
do not even allege that they were eye-witnesses
of the event they describe. Suppose the historian
averred that Cæsar never died, that he was still living
hundreds of years after his supposed assassination,
no matter how momentous the consequences which
had flowed from that belief, would we be satisfied
with ordinary proof of the fact? The alleged resurrection of Jesus is just as legitimate a problem of
scientific inquiry as any fact of geology or natural
history, because it is put forward as a concrete physical fact. Indeed, the whole Christian problem is
a historical problem, one of documents and records,
and falls within the reach of inductive research.
We may ask, Is it true? The impartial inquirer

will approach it in the true scientific spirit, weighing the probabilities, clearing up the discrepancies, and seeking verification. He will ask how far do the occurrences narrated square with the world of human experience? What was the type of mind, credulous or incredulous, realistic or imaginative? What were the current beliefs and expectations? How far does the imperfect knowledge of the times crop out in the narrative? How far do the current superstitions crop out? For instance, we see here in the Gospel writings a belief in angels, or supernatural human beings, and in demoniacal possessions cropping out. Has the subsequent experience of mankind confirmed or dissipated the belief in these things? We see in Matthew's narrative the belief that the dead sometimes come forth from their graves and walk abroad and appear to men, and that they choose darkness rather than light; we see the belief that dead saints and worthy persons may come back to earth, and we see everywhere an unquestioning belief in the reality of what we call miracles, or physical results brought about by other than physical means. Do these things agree with the rest of our knowledge? If not, is the proof of them commensurate with their exceptional character?

John Locke stated the truth about this matter of faith and reason two hundred years ago.

" There being many things," he says, " wherein

we have very imperfect notions, or none at all; and other things of whose past, present, or future existence, by the natural use of our faculties, we can have no knowledge at all; these as being beyond the discovery of our natural faculties, and above reason, are, when revealed, the proper matter of faith. Thus, that part of the angels rebelled against God, and thereby lost their first happy state; and that the dead shall rise and live again: these, and the like, being beyond the discovery of reason, are purely matters of faith, with which reason has directly nothing to do."

But Locke says that reason is to judge whether or not the revelation be genuine. Yet what test the reason has of the validity of a revelation the philosopher does not set forth.

If the facts or truths revealed are above reason, how can the fact of the revelation itself be proved to reason? Is faith itself reasonable? Of course it all depends upon the assumption with which we start. If we start with the assumption upon which the church is founded, namely, the assumption of an anthropomorphic God, an Infinite Person, the creator and upholder of all things, whose plans with reference to man have not gone smoothly, but have been sadly deranged and frustrated by man himself through what we call sin, so that the creature is hopelessly estranged from the creator, and so on through the rest of the theological formula, — if we start with this assumption, all the rest comes easy: faith and revelation are reasonable, the theory of the Christ and the atonement is reasonable, and with one or two more assumptions, which Cardinal Newman readily makes, the Catholic church becomes the very child and servant of reason. It is reasonable that this Infinite Person, who is not here upon earth, but in heaven, should want a representative, a vicar, in this world, to look after the well-being of his children, and what more reasonable than that the great mother church, the church which the apostles founded, should be that go-between, that representative? The Protestant churches are all more or less compromises with the devil, that is, with reason, with sense, with the natural man; but the Catholic church makes no compromises with the individual; it stands for authority. In fact, out of the purely human or anthropomorphic conception of the universe upon which our theology is based, it arises as the inevitable result. If your assumption at one end of the Christian scheme is reasonable, your acceptance of the Catholic church at the other is equally so. If the universe is an institution, a government, a hierarchy, and if mankind are in a lost and rebellious condition with reference to the head of this government or hierarchy, then does the idea of an infallible pope and all the saving ordinances of the church harmonize perfectly with this conception.

When you once assume the existence of the supernatural, you adjust your reason to that assumption. "If the supernatural exists," says a Catholic writer, "it is reasonable that it should exist; it is reasonable that it should present difficulties, that we should be able to apprehend it only in part, that we should need a special endowment of power or insight, called faith, to fully enter into it; it is reasonable that faith should not obliterate the inferior intellectual faculties, but should supplement and raise them; it is reasonable that there should be a revealed religion, and that this religion should possess mysteries."

St. Paul's definition of faith the religious mind has clung to very fondly, — namely, "the substance of things hoped for, the evidence of things not seen;" and Dr. Fisher's new version of the passage — to wit, "the firm assurance of things hoped for, the being convinced of things not seen" — can hardly take its place in the popular conscience. It is true, but not taking. Faith is neither evidence nor substance, though the religious world is constantly persuading itself that it is. "It makes real to the mind objects of hope" — so real that "they exercise a due control in the shaping of conduct."

As we have been long taught, belief in the Christian religion is more a matter of will than of reason. The will must be reached or enlisted first. Coleridge said to Crabb Robinson that "religious belief is an act, not of the understanding, but of the will. To become a believer one must love the doctrine and feel in harmony with it, and not sit down and coolly inquire whether he should believe it or not."

Hence I agree with Dr. Fisher that in these matters "the timidity of reason has to be overcome by a courageous exercise of will. In appropriating, or making our own, the things of faith, there is a venture to be made on the ground of evidence, without the stimulus and support of an appeal to the senses." People of strong wills, men of action and of affairs, are less apt to be skeptical than more purely meditative and intellectual minds. Wordsworth said of his poet, —

> " You must love him, ere to you
> He will seem worthy of your love; "

and of the Christian faith it is equally true that you must believe it ere it seems worthy of your credence. How to do this is the great problem. Hence the cry that goes up from the churches continually for more faith, more faith.

I have said that faith begins where reason ends; but by this statement I would only emphasize the fact that the province of the one lies entirely outside the province of the other. In the order of nature faith is first. We find ourselves in possession of a certain belief or certitude, and then we proceed to reason about it. In the order of historical development religion is not a matter of belief, of creeds and dogmas, but of observances. The early nations had certain religious rites and practices, but no belief, in our sense of the word; that is, as a conscious intellectual act. A man cannot reason himself into religion, though he can reason himself into religious opinions. Religion is a sentiment just as much as poetry is, and does not wait upon the logical faculties any more than poetry does. The demonstrations of science no competent mind can resist, but the demonstrations of religion, its proofs, and its evidences, only impress such minds as are already convinced, as have already taken the leap which faith requires.

Religious faith is losing ground in our day because the light which fills the world, begotten by science, education, industry, democracy, is more and more the light of broad noonday, clear, strong, merciless. Our fathers stood much nearer the twilight, the region of sentiment, of emotion, of enticing but delusive lights and shades. The morning of the world is past: what the completed day will show forth does not yet appear.

security in his mind, — these are of quite a different
nature, and our logical faculties can have little to do
with them.

Professor Huxley, in his " Nineteenth Century "
articles referred to, applies the scientific method of
inquiry to certain alleged occurrences in the New
Testament — occurrences which must rest upon
objective evidence, if upon any, and in which the
appeal of credibility is made, not to our faculty of
spiritual insight, but to our reason and understanding. Is the story of the Gadarene swine probable?
is it reasonable? does it agree with the rest of our
knowledge? " The Gadarene miracle either happened, or it did not. Whether the Gadarene ' question' is moral or religious or not has nothing to do
with the fact that it is a purely historical question
whether the demons said what they are declared to
have said, and the devil-possessed pigs did or did
not rush over the cliffs of the Lake of Gennesaret
on a certain day of a certain year." " If that is not
a matter about which evidence ought to be required,
and not only legal but strict scientific proof demanded by sane men who are asked to believe the
story — what is it?" Professor Huxley thinks a
man who believes such a story without logical evidence is guilty of an immoral act. And so generally
with the miracles recorded in the New Testament,
and with demonology and possessions. These things
are alleged occurrences in the outward physical

world, and they are not supported by adequate objective evidence.

Men reason upon the subject of the soul's immortality, but the answer which reason gives is mainly in the negative. There is nothing that could be called evidence that man continues to live after the dissolution of his body. Yet Dr. Abbott is convinced that he does so exist ; he realizes in himself " a nature superior to disease, decay, mortality ; " and who shall gainsay him ? who shall say he is illogical ? The evidence he has upon this point is personal and subjective, and cannot be imparted to another. It has no logical or scientific validity, because it begins and ends with himself. It is not a question of reason, but of religious conviction. But all the questions in dispute between Professor Huxley and Dr. Wace are questions of reason and of evidence. They pertain to the outward, visible, concrete world of history and of experience, and can be settled in no court but the court of reason.

Dr. Abbott says (and he assumes to speak for " the great mass of Christian believers ") " that there are propositions which men ought to believe without logically satisfying evidence." This is what the old mother church used to say, and used to back it up with the stake and the rack. " Ought to believe ; " that is, it is a man's duty to believe certain propositions addressed to his rational faculties, without rationally satisfying evidence. It is to be

99

regretted that the good doctor did not cite some theological or religious proposition, or some article from the creeds, that it is a man's duty thus to believe. Would he say that a man ought to believe any of the points in dispute between Professor Huxley and Dr. Wace without "logically satisfying evidence," — the swine story, the authorship of the Gospels, that Jesus said what he is reported to have said, that demonology is true?

Professor Huxley, I imagine, would be the last man in the world to deny Dr. Abbott's proposition that there is such a thing as spiritual insight, or the religious sense, and that certainties, or at least assurances and satisfaction, reach the soul through these avenues. The religious nature or the poetic and artistic nature is not occupied with logical processes or the reasons of things, but with impressions, attractions, intuitions, emotional processes, the divine, the beautiful, the enjoyable. We do not ask of a poem, or a work of art, or any work of pure literature, Is it true? as we would ask of a proposition of science, or the statement of a witness upon the stand, or the declaration of a creed, Is it true? but, Is it good? is it powerful? is it satisfying? does it move and nourish us? A poem must have poetic truth, but how different is this from mathematical or scientific truth, and by what different faculties apprehended! Neither do we ask of purely religious utterances like the Sermon on the Mount

or Paul's Epistles, Are they true? but, Do they
stimulate and exalt our religious sense? do they
quicken and purify the spirit? Paul's theology may
be true or false : what is forever true and real is his
fervid piety, his spiritual power, his eloquent humility, and his love for mankind. His logical faculties
may have been weak; the things which he believed,
which lay in his understanding and satisfied his
reason, may have been utterly inadequate to stand
rigid tests, but for all that the power and value of
his writings are beyond question. The same may
be said of some of the fathers of the church, weak
in reason, but strong in the spirit. Professor Huxley is strong in reason ; his logic is a chain hard to
break ; but highly spiritual and imaginative natures
would perhaps find little satisfaction in his writings. He is occupied with objective truth, not with
subjective impressions. His mind is strictly scientific, and the results of his method of inquiry are
hard to controvert.

He does not deny the moral sense, or the æsthetic
sense, or the religious sense, as Dr. Abbott would
seem to imply ; he is not discussing questions that
lie in either of these realms, but questions that
come within the scope of reason and are matters of
evidence. The questions of right and wrong in
human conduct, of lying, of stealing, of murder,
etc., which Dr. Abbott introduces, belong to quite
a different sphere from the question of the author-

101

ship of the Gospels or of the credibility of the miracles.

There is the appeal to conscience, the appeal to taste, the appeal to our sense of the fitness of things, and there is also the appeal to reason, to the judgment, to our power to weigh and sift evidence. It seems to me that Dr. Abbott confounds these things, and in his reply to Huxley sets up a man of straw. If the great scientist had said that all truth and certainty come through the logical faculties, he would have laid himself open to the doctor's criticism. What he did say or imply was that all scientific, all objective truth comes through our logical faculties. These are his words : " It is wrong for a man to say that he is certain of the objective truth of any proposition unless he can produce evidence which logically justifies that certainty."

In the outward objective world a fact is always a fact. It is always pertinent to inquire into the truth of any alleged occurrence. Did the sun stand still for Joshua to conquer his enemies? Is this a fact? If the sun stood still once it may stand still again. Do miracles happen? Have they ever happened? Is there a personal devil? Are we surrounded by a multitude of good and bad spirits who are seeking to influence our lives? Any objective evidence of the truth and reality of these things must hold good at all times and in all places. Two and two always make four, and doubtless always will. But when we enter the region of morals, we are in a world where all is plastic, indefinite, relative. Right and wrong are so only under certain conditions. It may be right to lie and steal and murder under certain extraordinary circumstances. "The certainties of the moral and spiritual realm " to which Dr. Abbott refers, and upon which he says "" all æsthetic, all domestic, all political and national life are based," are not outward demonstrable certainties, like those of science, but inward personal certainties, which involve our constitution and our temporary relations to the universe and to each other.

Dr. Abbott says he feels but a languid interest in the critical discussion as to the authorship of the four Gospels. This may well be. It may be because Dr. Abbott is not primarily interested in questions of evidence or in logical and reasoning processes. He is a moralist and preacher, and seeks the springs of conduct, not the sources of logical conviction. I believe he accepts the doctrine of demoniacal possession ; it seems to suit his emotional and imaginative type of mind. But a man of science, as such, could no more accept such an explanation of any form of insanity than he could attribute crystallization to the work of fairies or the wind and the storm to furies. The authorship of the four Gospels may not be a vital question to the religious mind, but as a question it is a matter of evidence, and not at all of personal impression.

If Christianity really rested upon evidence, if its vitality was solely dependent upon verifiable facts and considerations, like a work of science, it would have perished from the earth long ago. But it does not live by its so-called evidences. Christianity is largely a matter of the heart, of the feelings and the emotions. It has not rested upon logical evidences; its main hold in the first instance has not been upon men's scientific faculties, but upon their hopes, fears, aspirations, and spiritual cravings. To talk about the reasonableness of Christianity is like talking about the reasonableness of magic or witchcraft. The human faculties are utterly powerless before its main tenets. Christianity has the vitality of literature, of poetry and art. The Gospel records have wonderful, even magical, power as literature. They are true, not as history, but as poetry.

The myth of the resurrection will be kept alive for ages to come, notwithstanding all that has been or can be urged against it, because mankind have such a profound interest in believing it.

Christianity does not offer a system of philosophy, but a religious incentive. When it attempts to play the rôle of interpreter of the visible order of the universe, or to satisfy our rational faculties, its failure is pathetic ; its proofs are childish ; its science is essentially pagan ; its story of the fall as an explanation of the origin of evil and its " plan of salvation " as a means of escape from that evil, as science, do not rise above any of the delusions of the pagan world. The story of the Chaldee god, Bel, who cut off his own head, moistened the clay with his blood, and then made man out of it, is just as rational an explanation of the origin of man as the one the Christian church has always adhered to. In fact, the whole basis of our theology, the conception of Jesus as a supernatural person who had no earthly father, and who rose from the dead and ascended bodily up into heaven, is essentially pagan, and belongs to an order of things that has long since passed away. The power of Christianity is a spiritual power; it is in its appeals to the ideal of the gentle, the merciful, the meek, the forgiving, the pure in heart, — an ideal which has such an attraction for the European nations, — and also to the love of reward and the fear of punishment which materialistic ages foster. In one is its charm for fine natures; in the other its power over the multitude.

Theological writers are in general prone to magnify subjective certitude at the expense of objective proof; to place faith above reason, in the domain of reason. They sneer at science and logic as if in their sphere they could be dispensed with and something else be substituted in their place. Thus Professor Blackie, in that vituperative book of his, "The Natural History of Atheism," — a book the style of which is like a man going through a house and banging the doors behind him, — says, as a finishing stroke to the "drivel" of our "boastful science," that the "highest cognitions are never reached by the mere exercise of the knowing faculties, on whatever subject exercised." Not even, I suppose, when exercised upon the multiplication table! "Instinct and aspiration," he goes on to say, "are higher than knowledge; and the pretensions of the merely scientific man to assume the dictatorship of things that be are not founded on nature. Many things can be known only by being felt; all vital forces are fundamentally unknowable, but they exist not the less because would-be philosopher B or would-be philosopher C has no machinery with which to measure or control them." Are instinct and aspiration "cognitions"? Do they belong to the sphere of knowledge? Do they even point to any certain and demonstrable conclusions? They may or they may not be higher than knowledge; it is certain that they cannot take the place of knowledge. Instinct and aspiration enlightened by knowledge is the desirable order, is it not? The only thing the scientific man assumes is that the scientific method is the only proper one with which to deal with the objective world of fact and experience. If the professor meant to say that some things are to be felt and not known, he is near the truth. The facts of science are to be known; we may know Kepler's laws; we can hardly feel them, since they are not personal.

But truths of art, of poetry, of religion, are to be felt, whether we known them or not. They come to us by a synthetical, not by an analytical process.

I have no disposition to overrate our mere knowing faculties; I only want to say that what we *know* we know through them. What we feel or fancy or hope forms no part of our true knowledge, and may come through other avenues. The perception of the beautiful is not a part of our knowledge; neither is the perception of the moral or the spiritual. These things are from within; they are subjective and not objective, and not within the range of the scientific faculties. They are real, just as pleasure and pain are real; they are experiences of the mind. The whole sphere of religion lies here; the kingdom of heaven is within you, not in some outward relation or condition.

Neither do I wish to imply that there is any feud between science and true religion, between that part of man's nature which thirsts for exact knowledge — the red rays of the spectrum, so to speak — and that part of his nature which we call the spiritual, and which fades off into the vast unknown — the violet rays, at the other extreme; nor between either of these and his æsthetic nature, his love of beautiful forms, though in different individuals these different parts will not be equally developed, nor will they be equally active in different races and times. The feud is between true science and false science, between the conception of an order that is rational and one that is irrational, between modern pathology and Indian "medicine."

Exact science deals with and can only deal with the objective, the rigid, inexorable world of law. With the subjective, the world within us, the world of personality, whence comes all we call literature, art, religion, philosophy, it cannot deal. Here exact demonstration is not possible ; all is plastic, growing, conflicting, aspiring, indeterminate. The personal element modifies everything. The laws by which insensate bodies act and react upon each other may be determined, but the laws by which persons act and react upon each other are quite another matter. In the subjective world truth is relative, but in the world of science truth is absolute. Chemical elements always combine in the same proportions; moisture is always precipitated from the air under the same conditions; the operations of physical nature are uniform; given the same conditions, and the same results always follow. Doubtless the same results always follow the same conditions in the world of mind and personality also, but here the conditions are more obscure and more fluctuating, and science cannot grasp them.

Every original mind may have, and usually does have, a philosophy of its own, a religion of its own, a political creed of its own, literary preferences of its own; but every mind cannot have a science of its own. The personal element is alien to science. How many systems of philosophies have there been from Aristotle down to Spencer? How many times have the old problems been explained? But one man's science must be another man's science; all science is a whole — a pushing farther and farther of the lines of knowledge into nature.

The hostility between the scientific and the spiritual, or the truly religious, may well cease, if, indeed, there ever has been, or ever can be, real hostility. We are bound to give the reason and the understanding full sway in their own proper fields. In subduing and in utilizing this world, or adjusting ourselves to it, we have no guide but science. Yet science is not the main part of life, notwithstanding all the noise it is making in the world. Science is making a great noise in the world because it is doing a great work. Literature, art, religion, speculation, have had their day; that is, the highest achievements of which they are capable are undoubtedly of the past. But science is young; it is now probably only in the heat of its forenoon work. It is a little curious that man's knowing faculties, the first to be appealed to, should be the latest in maturing; that he should worship so profoundly, admire so justly, act so wisely and heroically, while he yet knew so little accurately of the world in which he was placed, Does not this fact point to the conclusion that science is not the main part of

THE LIGHT OF DAY

life? It is probably the main part of our material
civilization, of that by which we are clothed and
fed and warmed and transported, defended in war
and housed in peace; but of an intrinsic civilization it forms a less part. The old Greek had little
or no material civilization in the modern sense; his
civilization was personal and mental. What distin-
guishes the modern man is not his personal superi-
ority, but the enormous engines and deft appliances
with which he is fended and armed, and the great-
ness of his material triumphs.

Yet knowledge is not discredited, reason is not
supplanted. We can no more dispense with them
than we can dispense with the bones in our bodies.
They furnish the framework by which our lives are
upheld. All the certainty we have of the order of
the objective world comes through our rational faculties.

The agnostic does not merely say that all knowledge is imperfect and fragmentary, nor that all
certainty is based on the logical faculty; but simply
that the understanding goes upon evidence; that in
this world we have no guide to objective truth but
our rational faculties. He finds no room for what
our religious brethren call faith, because faith, as
commonly understood, is a fatal undertow that
swamps and drowns reason. He finds many things
and enjoys many things which he cannot understand; he is not a stranger to the thrill of awe and

110

reverence in the presence of the great mystery of the universe; but all propositions relative to the plans, ways, and nature of that mystery that are not verifiable, he fights shy of.

VII

THE MODERN SKEPTIC

A RECENT writer upon skepticism describes the skeptic as generally a "malcontent," not only in religion, but in politics and in society. "He is the personification of the ancient belief regarding the souls of the unburied dead," that is, he goes wandering about homeless and disconsolate. But few honest skeptics, I imagine, will see themselves in this portrait. The religious skeptics of to-day are a very large class, larger than ever before, and they are by no means the restless and unhappy set they are here described. On the contrary they are among the most hopeful, intelligent, patriotic, upright, and wisely conservative of our citizens. Let us see; probably four fifths of the literary men in this country and in Great Britain, and a still larger per cent on the Continent, are what would be called skeptics; a large proportion of journalists and editors are skeptics; half the lawyers, more than half the doctors, a large per cent of the teachers, a large per cent of the business men, almost all the scientific men, and a great many orthodox clergymen, if they were to avow their real convictions, would confess

113

to some shade of skepticism or religious unbelief. They find the creeds in which they were nurtured no longer credible. Indeed, there are but few great names in literature, in science or philosophy, for a hundred years, that could not be convicted of some shade of religious skepticism,— skepticism about the miracles, the sacraments, vicarious atonement, original sin, or some other dogma.

The lawyers are probably less inclined to skepticism than the doctors, because the legal mind is closer akin to the theological mind; it has chiefly to do with arbitrary and artificial questions and distinctions, and is brought less under the influence of natural causes than that of the medical practitioner. The lawyer falls into personal and *ex parte* views; he makes the cause of his client his own; and his whole training is to beget a habit of mind quite the opposite of the scientific. The physicians were the first to discredit witchcraft and to write against it, but the lawyers cherished and defended the belief nearly as long as did the clergy. The legalism, too, which has invaded Christianity, and which is such a repulsive feature in certain of the creeds, especially that of Calvinism, is the work of the attorney habit of mind.

The writer referred to is correct, however, in saying that " faith is a living force mostly in active temperaments." There is less skepticism among the farmers and among the laboring classes generally, except maybe here and there in large cities, and very little among the women. Women are slow to reason, but quick to feel and to believe, and they cannot face the chill of the great cosmic out of doors without being clad in some tangible faith. The mass of the people are indifferent rather than skeptical. They are undoubtedly drifting away from the creeds of their fathers, but they have not yet entirely lost sight of them. "The various modes of worship which prevailed in the Roman world," says Gibbon, "were all considered by the people as equally true; by the philosopher as equally false, and by the magistrate as equally useful." This is probably very much the case amid all nations, at all times.

Men of large action, too, generals, statesmen, sea captains, explorers, usually share the religion of their contemporaries. Frederick the Great is perhaps the most notable exception to this rule. A popular religion is always definite and practical, clothes itself in concrete forms, and appeals to the active temperament. The man of action has little time for reflection, to return upon himself and entertain intellectual propositions. Faith is an earlier and in many ways a healthier act of the mind than reason, because faith leads to action, while reason makes us hesitate and put off a decision. The church has always had trouble with philosophers and physicians, with men who wanted to know the reason of things and trace the connection of cause and effect. There was little skepticism in Greece until after the sophists appeared, the critics, men of ideas, who directed a free play of thought upon all objects and subjects, a type of mind which begat the philosophers of Athens, but not the great poets and artists. They came earlier, when there was more faith and less reason in Greece.

In fact, the great days of Greece were not when its head was the clearest, but when its patriotism and religion were the most fervent. As the heart cools the head clears. Those great emotional uprisings, those religious enthusiasms, which come in time to all nations, are not days of right reason nor of correct science ; still they are the periods of history we like best to dwell upon.

It is always easier to believe than to deny. Our minds are naturally affirmative ; it is not till the second or third thought that doubt begins. Belief is so vital and necessary that one would say the tendency was made strong at the perpetual risk of extra belief and superstition ; it were better to believe too much than not enough. Hence mankind has always believed too much, as if to make sure that the anchor hold. To believe just enough, to free his mind from all cant and from all illusion, and see things just as in themselves they are, is the aim of the philosopher or of the true skeptic.

Men's minds are nearly always under a spell of

some kind. What a spell the mind of Europe was under during the Crusades! What a foolish and misdirected enthusiasm this uprising seems to us, whose minds are under some other spell, say the scientific spell! What a spell the same mind was under for centuries with reference to witchcraft, even such a man as Sir Matthew Hale believing in it and defending it! Here was an astute legal mind, and an incorruptible judge, a man who could sift evidence and expose a false witness, and yet the spell of his times in regard to witchcraft was upon him, and he could not escape it. The mind reasons in such cases, but it reasons inside of a magical circle, the bounds of which it cannot pass, cannot see. Most of us reason inside of a circle, when we reason at all, with reference to our religion; we are under its spell, its illusion. What a spell the mind of Christendom has been under with reference to miracles — could not get or see beyond the magic circle. The Catholic mind is still under this spell. What a spell the mind of the world was under in the third and fourth centuries with reference to magic, and in later times with reference to astrology and alchemy and demoniac possessions! The skeptic sees how faith or belief tends perpetually to fulfill itself. If I believed in ghosts I should doubtless see ghosts. People always have. Those who believe in spiritism have wonderful things to relate; but to a cool, unbiased person not one scrap of

into a decline, and soon dies. Thus faith kills and faith cures. Faith in your physician is often worth more to you than his medicines; a soldier's faith in his general doubles or trebles his force.

The skeptic sees the benefits of a strong, active faith, irrespective of the object toward which it is directed. Faith in one's self and in the justice of one's cause is always half the battle. It is not for nothing that we have had so long thundered into our ears the benefits of belief and the dangers of skepticism and doubt. And it is not because the things we have been asked to believe are in themselves true, but because the very act of belief is in itself wholesome and sets the current going, while doubt paralyzes and leads to stagnation. But how shall we believe a thing unless we know it to be true? Ah, there is the rub! But man in all ages has been the victim of delusions, and the gain to him has been that they have kept him going ; that they have kept him working and striving. The great periods in history have been periods of strong faith, of serious affirmation, not of denial, nor yet of reason. Yet I would not say that faith alone has ever made a people or an individual great. Spain, as a nation, probably has as much faith as ever, and yet how is she fallen from the three hundred years ago ! But faith is more frequently the parent of great deeds than reason or denial. From the point of view of the nation, faith is best. There can be

119

no strong feeling of nationality without a certain
narrowness and unreasonableness. The philosophers of Athens no doubt weakened the feeling
of nationality. They weakened the faith in the
nation's gods ; they had reference to universal
ends. A proud, intense, exclusive nation like the
Hellenes had a kind of faith in itself and in its
privileges and destiny, which, however conducive
to the growth and strength of the nation, could
not stand the light of reason and universal knowledge.

The wise skeptic also sees that faith or superstition, rather than reason, must be the guide of the
mass of mankind. What Strabo said nineteen centuries ago still holds true. "It is impossible," said
the old Greek, "to conduct women and the gross
multitude, and to render them holy, pious, and upright by the precepts of reason and philosophy ;
superstition or the fear of the gods must be called
in aid, the influence of which is founded on fiction
or prodigies. For the thunder of Jupiter, the ægis
of Minerva, the trident of Neptune, the torches and
snakes of the Furies, the spears of the gods adorned
with ivy, and the whole ancient theology are all
fables which the legislators who formed the political
constitution of states employ as bugbears to over-
awe the credulous and simple."

But from the point of view of the individual, of a
serene, well-balanced, well-ordered life, reason is the

best. "Prove all things, hold fast that which is good," is the voice of the cool, disinterested reason, directed to the individual. And when one sets out to prove all things, what guide can he have other than reason? This is "the light that lighteth every man that cometh into the world," — this and conscience; but in the region of speculative opinion and belief, conscience plays a very subordinate part. "To reconcile theory and fact," says Cardinal Newman, "is almost an instinct of the mind." It certainly is in our day ; more so, probably, than ever before. No intelligent man can now conscientiously humble his reason before his faith, as good Sir Thomas Browne boasted he could. He said, "Men that live according to the right rule and law of reason, live but in their own kind, as brutes do in theirs." He said we are to believe, "not only above but contrary to reason and against the argument of our proper senses." A good many other people believed so too about that time. Poor Ann Arkens — young, intelligent, and beautiful — was stretched upon the rack, then burned with fagots and blown with gunpowder at Smithfield, all because she could not believe, against the "argument of her proper senses," in transubstantiation, that the bread and wine the priest had mumbled over remained anything but bread and wine.

The skepticism of our day is mainly the result of science, of the enormous growth of our natural

knowledge. In its light the old theology and cosmology look artificial and arbitrary; they do not fit
into the scheme of creation as science discloses it.
Our science is undoubtedly ignorant enough. We
know no more about final causes, after science has
done its best, than we did before, but familiarity
with the laws and processes of the world does undoubtedly beget a habit of mind unfavorable to the
personal and arbitrary view of things which the
old theology has inculcated. Science has at least
taught us that the universe is all of a piece, or homogeneous; that man is a part of nature; that there
are no breaks or faults in the scheme of creation,
and can be none. One thing follows from another or
is evolved from another, the whole system of things
is vital, and not mechanical, and nothing is interpolated or arbitrarily thrust in from without. All
our natural knowledge is based upon these principles.
It is only in theology that we encounter notions that
run counter to them, and that require our acceptance
of doctrines in which our powers of reason and observation can have no part.

The man of science has no trouble in discover-
ing God objectively; that is, as the all-embracing
force and vitality that pervades and upholds the
physical universe — in fact, he can discover little
else. Knock at any door he will, he finds the Eternal
there to answer. But his search discloses no human
attributes, nothing he can name in the terms he ap-

While this inward revelation of God to the spirit may be the most convincing of all proofs to the person experiencing it, yet it can have little force with another, little force as an argument, because, in the first place, it cannot be communicated or demonstrated. All independent objective truth is capable of being communicated and of being verified; but this fact of which Newman is so certain, he confesses himself, he cannot bring out with any logical force. It is its own proof. And in the second place, because the world knows how delusive these personal impressions and inward voices are. Men have heard an inward voice or felt an inward prompting that has led them to commit the most outrageous crimes against humanity, — to burn witches and heretics, to mortify their own bodies, or to throw themselves from precipices. Good men and wise men have been equally sure, upon subjective evidence, of the existence of the devil; they have heard his promptings, his suggestions, and they have fought against him. Our fathers were just as sure, upon personal grounds, of the existence of the devil as Newman is of the existence of God. One may personify the whisperings or the motives of evil within himself, and give it a bad name, and he may personify the nobler and higher voices within him and give it a good name. In either case it is a subjective phenomenon, which the man bent upon exact knowledge cannot attach much weight to.

124

Satan walked and talked with the biblical writers, the same as did God; he even talked face to face with God himself. Not long since a respectable mechanic in one of the large cities believed himself bewitched; the delusion worked upon him till he took to his bed, and finally he actually died, to all intents and purposes bewitched to death.

It is in the light of such facts and considerations as these that the so-called skeptic refuses to credit all people tell him about their knowledge of God. So that he is finally compelled to rest upon the God of force and law of outward nature.

It is also to be said that the decay of religious belief in our times is rather a decay of creeds and dogmas than of the spirit of true religion — religion as love, as an aspiration after the highest good. If we regard it as a decay of Christianity itself, it is to be remembered that Christianity bears no such intimate relation to modern life, either the life of the individual or to the life of the state, as polytheism bore to the life of the ancient world. It is rather of the nature of an aside in modern life, while in Greece and Rome and in Judea the national religion was the principal matter. The whole drama of history clustered around and was the illustration of this central fact. The state and the church were one. The national gods were invoked and deferred to on all occasions. Every festival was in honor of some divinity; the public games were presided over by some god. In going to war or in concluding peace, solemn sacrifices were offered and the favor of the gods was solicited.

In fact, in the ancient world there was but one principle, — the religious principle. This dominated everything, — science, literature, the arts, the state, the nation, the individual; everything revolved about and was subordinated to this rule. Men lived on the most familiar terms with the supernatural powers. In Mohammedan countries there is still but one principle. But among the European nations the religious principle is but one of two; it is relegated to the sects, and is aired once a week. The mass of modern life is secular and not religious. The modern state is not even decently moral. The attitude of the great European powers toward each other to-day is precisely that of so many dogs growling at each other over their bones.

"The religion of polytheism," says Gibbon, "was not merely a speculative doctrine professed in the schools or preached in the temples." On the contrary, its deities and its rites "were closely interwoven with every circumstance of business or pleasure, of public or private life."

In comparison with many Oriental peoples we are an irreligious and God-forsaken nation. No gods are recognized by the state, and in 1796 Washington signed a treaty with a Mohammedan country, in which it was declared that "the government of the

United States is not in any sense founded on the Christian religion."

Hence, whatever we owe to Christianity, we cannot begin to owe to it what the ancient peoples owed to their religions. Great Britain still maintains the union of church and state, but it is a forced and artificial union; it is a *union* and not a *oneness*, a matter of law and not of life, as in ancient times. Yet ours is an age of faith, too, — faith in science, in the essential soundness and goodness of the world. We are skeptical about the gods, but we are no longer skeptical about things, or about duty, or virtue, or manliness, or the need of well-ordered lives. The putting out of the candles on the altar has not put out the sun and stars too. We affirm more than we deny. We no longer deny the old religions, but accept them and see where they belong. Man is fast reaching the point where he does not need these kinds of props and stays, the love of future good or the fear of future evil. There was a time when the pulling down of the temple pulled the sky down with it, all motives for right were extinguished; but that time is past. Righteousness has a scientific basis; the anger of heaven descends upon the ungodly in the shape of penalties for violated laws. A comet in the heavens is no longer a fearful portent, but sewer gas in your house is. Cholera is not a visitation for ungodliness, but for uncleanliness, which is a form of ungodliness. We cannot

127

pray with the old faith, but we can fight intemperance with more than the old zeal. We cannot love God as our fathers did, but we can love our neighbor much more. The spirit of charity and helpfulness has increased in the world as the old beliefs have declined. The skeptics and disbelievers could never slaughter each other as the Christians have. Science substitutes a rational basis for right conduct in place of the artificial basis of the church. The anger of the gods no longer threatens us; the displeasure of the church is no longer a dread; but we know that virtue alone brings satisfaction. We cannot read the Bible with the old eyes, but we read nature with new eyes.

Probably religion has long ceased to play any important part in the great movements of the world. A religious war is no longer possible. In our two great wars and in the founding of this republic, religious belief was not concerned at all. The skeptics were just as ardent and just as brave and patriotic as the believers. The author of the Declaration of Independence was a skeptic. The policy of England, France, Germany, Russia, is it in any way inspired by the Christian religion? Never were so much courage and hope and benevolence and virtue in the world as to-day, and never before were the ties of the old faiths so weak.

VIII

THE DECADENCE OF THEOLOGY

THE death of Tennyson the other day with a copy of Shakespeare in his hand instead of the Bible or the Prayer Book, and with only his family and physician by his bedside, does not seem to have sent any shudder through the orthodox religious world. That a great poet in his last moments should seek to lean upon the spirit of another great poet, gone before, is natural enough; too natural, one would think, to suit the supernaturalists. Tennyson's was a profoundly religious nature, but evidently he had worked his way out of the quagmire of the theological creeds. It was a significant deathbed, science watching the body and literature ministering to the soul. Where the parish priest was we are not told; men's thoughts in their last hours are turning less and less to him. The faith that really saves, saves from an ignoble terror that impoverishes life and makes death hideous, is no longer in the keeping of our theological doctors. Renan passed away with far more cheerfulness and composure, if reports be true, than did Cardinal Manning. The serenity of Renan, as he said of his friend Calmann, "was that of a good man, sure of

being in accord with superior rule." Renan seems
to have written his last book, "Recollections and
Letters," with the thought of death ever present
with him, yet the gayety of it, the buoyancy and
sweetness, are remarkable.

The atmosphere of our time is fast being cleared
of the fumes and deadly gases that arose during the
carboniferous age of theology. Renan has been one
of the forces, with his divine gayety and serene reason, that has helped dispel them. Professor Huxley, in his recent volume of essays and discourses,
drives them before him like a gale from the mountains. It would hardly seem possible for any self-
respecting theologian to again stand up for what is
called the historicity of the New Testament miracles.
Yet there be those who look upon all this with un-
easiness and distrust.

"Is the spiritual sense decadent?" asks one of
our current religious journals, meaning by the spiritual sense the faculty to discern the truth of the
current religious dogmas. The writer is forced to
the conclusion that this sense is weakening, but he
takes refuge in the thought that the objects of faith
are like the stars in the sky which the sun (science)
may obscure, but cannot blot out. He says the ag-
nosticism of Huxley and his kind is but the confession of a child that it cannot see by morning light
the moon which it saw at bedtime. The argument
of the religious editor frankly admits that there is

light in the world, and that it is no temporary or uncertain rushlight either, but the light of the real heavenly luminary itself. Sunlight is from above, too, is it not? and quite as needful, though not quite as bewitching and misleading as moonlight or starlight. The objects of faith may be real and again they may not; the proof is wanting. At any rate, it is at last daylight in the world, and the lights that are obscured or that fade away and are lost, it seems to me, we can very well do without. We shall never again believe in angels, or demoniacal possessions, or in witchcraft, or in spooks, or in spirit rappings, or in charms and incantations, or in the lake of fire, or in the city of the golden streets. In this morning of the world man is no longer the child that cried for the moon of the night before.

The analogy suggested by our religious editor is no doubt a true one; the difference between our times and the times of our fathers is mainly in the greater light of our day, the light of exact science. We see things as they are; we see how and where the delusions of the past arose, that they were incident to the general obscurity, that these portentous forms that were so real and threatening to our fathers are either shadows or harmless inanimate objects. No doubt we have lost something, — something in the direction of poetry and religion, the anthropomorphic gift. Man cannot make the world in his own image, or project himself into it as in the pre-scientific ages. Nature is not so plastic and neutral in the light of the sun as under the light of the moon. The day has its own obscurities and illusions, but they are not those of the night. Things take on less portentous forms; the eye and not the imagination rules. What power there is in mere darkness or obscurity itself! Take a person of unenlightened mind and see what things he will accept, simply because they are mysterious and transcend experience. In my youth the belief in ghosts, haunted houses, witches, signs and warnings, was almost universal among country people; now there is hardly a vestige of such belief left. The change indicated is not merely a change of weather, as Cardinal Newman thought; it is more than that, — it is the passing of one geological period into another.

The world is real, and goes its own way. The poet has a harder problem before him; the priest has a harder problem before him, but the men who are to do the world's real work find the problem much easier, — I mean the men who are to clothe, and feed, and shelter, and warm, and transport it; who are to fight its battles and subdue and reclaim its waste places. Science has its own mysteries and sublimities, and they have this advantage — they are real; they are not the reflection of the mood or the fancy of the observer; they are not the result of obscurity, but of the limitations of the human mind. Knowledge outstrips imagination.

Feeling, emotion, falls helpless before the revelations of science. The heights and the depths that surround us, and the world of vital forces in which our lives are embosomed, and which the darkness of earlier ages did not permit us to see, baffle speech. Magnitude, perspective, order, system, connection, is what the light of science reveals to us. How much sentiment, how much poetry and religion we can read in these things depends upon us. The nearness, the privacy, the fireside charm, and the dark-closet fear of nature are gone; in short, its purpose, its affection or hatred, as directed to you and me. The universe is going its own way with no thought of us; to keep in its currents is our life, to cross them is our death. This discovery sends the cosmic chill, with which so many of us are familiar in these days; it makes the religious mind gasp for breath, but we must face it, and still find life sweet under its influence. The world is not yet used to the open air of this thought — the great out of doors of it; we are not hardened to it. We have been so long housed in our comfortable little anthropomorphic creeds, with their artificial warmth and light, that when we are suddenly turned out of doors by this thought, we experience, I say, the cosmic chill. It is quite probable that future generations, with a more robust religious sense than ours, will have quite a different feeling in the presence of this discovery.

Behold what a chill, or series of chills, the religious mind has all along felt under the influence of the revelations of science, medicine, geology, astronomy! All have convulsed the religious mind. Evolution set the teeth of both priests and laymen chattering, and many of them are chattering still. Those who have been acclimated to the thought find new inspiration in it; their religious sense is more vigorous than before. It is like new blood poured into depleted veins.

It is beyond dispute that of the two rival or conflicting conceptions of the universe now pretty familiar to all current readers, the scientific conception and the theological conception, the one is waning, or becoming feebler day by day, the other growing stronger day by day. Up to the sixteenth or seventeenth century the theological conception held almost complete possession of man's mind. Only here and there did a bold thinker like Bruno or Roger Bacon chafe under its sway. But in our time the theological conception has been so modified by science that it is hardly recognizable any more. In the simplest and most liberal form this conception is embodied in the Mosaic account of creation. The universe was created out of nothing by God, man was made out of the dust of the earth, and woman out of man. Heaven was above the earth and Hades below. The world was the centre of the universe and the chief object in it. All the heavenly bodies revolved around it, the sun to give it light and warmth by day, the moon to give light by night. Then came the fall of Adam through the machinations of the devil, the beginning of evil, the expulsion from Paradise, the wrath and disappointment of God, the wholesale drowning, Noah and his ark, the chosen people, the new departure, the birth of Jesus, the plan of redemption, and the rest of the history which we know so well, and the curious arbitrary and unnatural and fortuitous character of it all.

There are probably very few theologians or religious thinkers of any sort in our day who still hold intact this original theological conception. It has been modified by the scientific conception, crowded back and lopped off here and there till but few of its main features remain. When it fully possessed men's minds, as during the long stretch of the theological ages, it cropped out in and colored every department of life and thought. Every event, every fact of history and experience, and every phenomenon of nature was seen through the medium of this conception. Out of it grew the belief in magic, alchemy, astrology, witchcraft, demoniacal possessions, sorcery, apparitions, miracles, charms, exorcisms. These notions fitted perfectly with the theological conception, — the conception of a world made and ruled by an anthropomorphic being. The belief in a devil or evil spirit upon whom to saddle all the mischief and disease and disasters became a necessity. How could a benevolent being do or permit these things? A devil must be had, even if we have to make one. Indeed, as soon as man invented an anthropomorphic God an anthropomorphic devil became a necessity. Think of the time when men really believed in the devil — when they did not simply believe that they believed in him, as we do nowadays, but when they believed in him as really as they believed in heat and cold, night and day, life and death; when doctors and theologians guarded their mouths while exorcising an evil spirit lest he jump down their throats. If a man inhaled a little fly by accident, his reason might be unhinged by terror lest he had swallowed the devil. The king of Spain used to sleep between the monks to keep the devil off. What a dreadful hue was given to life by this belief; in what a constant state of apprehension and alarm men lived! The insane, the epileptic were of course possessed of the devil. All evil, storms, pestilence, disease, everything malodorous, was the work of evil spirits.

When the scientific conception began to awaken in many minds, not a step could it take, or cause to be taken, without a collision with the theological conception or its brood of hateful offspring. Every domain was occupied. Disease, insanity, epilepsy, pestilence, storms, comets, fossils, malformations, all had their theological explanations. The scientific idea found itself opposed at every point. Hence arose the warfare of science with theology, which is a thrice-told tale. Lecky has written it in his history of Rationalism, Draper has written it, Andrew White has written it, and is lately adding his "New Chapters." Not one foothold has science gained without a struggle. Not one province has theology given up till it was compelled to. But step by step it has been forced to retreat, till at least four fifths of its territory is now occupied by its great rival. Magic and sorcery and alchemy and astrology are given up as idle dreams; witchcraft and hobgoblins and even the good devil are delusions of our fathers. The belief in miracles is narrowed down, among Protestants, to a very small span of history, namely, the New Testament miracles, and even these will probably soon be given up. The medical practitioner no longer uses charms or amulets of fantastic remedies; he is no longer fighting against evil spirits or seeking to thwart the will of God. The belief in the devil theory of insanity only lingers here and there in a few minds. The president of one of our colleges lately declared, in print, his belief in the theory. Some of the religious journals have protested against the late experiments of the government to compel rain, showing a remnant of the old theological idea that rain is a special providence. Probably the same type of mind is shocked at the audacity of the lightning-rod man; to be consistent it ought to discountenance the umbrella man as well, since to shed the electric fluid by aid of the

137

lightning rod seems no more irreligious than to shed the aqueous fluid by aid of the umbrella. The government agents found men in Virginia who had religious scruples about spraying their grapes against the black rot, and many good people still hold to special providences in their daily lives. Prayer, especially for material good, is a survival of the old theological concept. But for all practical purposes, in medicine, in geology, in astronomy, in the daily ordering of our lives, and in the springs of our natural civilization, the theological conception has been overthrown and the scientific conception has taken its place. We no longer tremble at an eclipse or at a comet, nor see in the northern lights the gleam of the fires of hell. We have learned something of the laws of storms and the causes of pestilence, and have found that cleanliness is a better safeguard against fever than fasting or prayer.

But what is the scientific conception of the universe? The idea in its simplest form is implied when we say that such and such an event or such and such a course of conduct is according to nature, or else is against nature, thereby recognizing the fact that there is an inherent order or sequence in the course of natural events. To find out this order and formulate it is the object of science, and leads to the scientific conception of the universe. To adjust our lives to it and avail ourselves of it is the success of our material civilization. In this conception the material universe is self-existent, self-governed, without beginning and without end, having no limits in time nor bounds in space. It leads us to the conviction that the sum of physical forces is constant, that the laws of causation and the conservation of energy are everywhere operative, but without initiation and without finality. There is the same difficulty in placing limits to time that there are in placing limits to space. Both are unthinkable. The annihilation of matter and the creation of matter *ex nihilo* are alike unthinkable. The man of science finds the order of nature rational, that effects are always linked with causes, that uniformity is never broken, that nothing is interpolated but follows in due course, — in short, that evolution and not special creation is the key to the universe. It follows that man is of animal origin, that he is fitted to his environment rather than it to him, that Nature befriends and furthers him when he obeys her laws, and crushes him when he crosses them. Science knows no other plan of redemption than the survival of the fittest, knows no other day of creation than this day, knows no other fall of man save the present daily fall of ignorance and vice, knows no heaven or hell save that we make for ourselves, knows no immortality save the persistence of life and force, and finally knows no God save the Infinite Power that fills and upholds all things.

Science does not prove that miracles or the supernatural are impossible, but it begets in the mind a conception of the universe which finds no place for these things. It discloses a harmony and a completeness which leaves no room for alien and extraneous forces. It is a complete solvent of the old notions. Theology recognized it as its mortal enemy at once, and has fought it inch by inch. Every generalization of science has been so much territory wrested from theology. What a blow to it was the Copernican system of astronomy! How Newton cut under it with his law of gravitation, how Darwin with his theory of the origin of species! It has been shorn of its influence like the Pope of his temporal power; it is confined almost entirely to the region of the unverifiable, and here it is safe. It may hurl its anathemas at the man of science, it may grant or refuse future probation to the heathen, it may consign the pagan philosophers to purgatory, it may damn infants or indorse murderers, it may call itself Calvinism or Methodism or Catholicism or Millerism, and the time spirit will look on content. Any spiritual influence it may still have over the masses, any power to brighten and elevate men's lives, science can thoroughly appreciate. But even the spiritual power of our theological Pope is waning fast. His anathemas no longer inspire terror, his blessings are no longer worth the journey to Rome for. In its chosen realm theology is little more than the vestige of its former self.

140

The principle of the unity and completeness of nature, or this perception of nature as an entity, a thing in and of itself, is comparatively a recent evolution. Our fathers had it but feebly, our remote theological ancestors not at all. But there is a growing conviction in the human mind to-day that the forces of nature are constant and adequate to all the phenomena of the visible world, and that there is no room and never has been any room for the introduction of forces extra-natural. Akin to this, and a part of it, is the feeling that any system of religion to be credible must be in line with the rest of our knowledge. That we apprehend moral, philosophical, artistic, and scientific truth with our normal faculties, but religious truth with a faculty that is a special gift from some power above us and that is not in any way related to the former, is a view hostile to the scientific synthesis. Our spiritual knowledge cannot contradict our natural knowledge. Faith must supplement, not forestall reason. If the law of evolution is not continuous, and if it is not adequate to cover the whole field of human development, religious as well as scientific, then we must find some law that is.

We make a monstrosity of creation when we make it half natural and half supernatural. If religion is something that has only an accidental relation to a man's natural capacity for goodness, and sin something which has only an accidental relation to his

141

natural defects and shortcomings, then are those things contradictory of the rest of our knowledge. Why the man of science has difficulty with the current faith is because it will not fit in with the scheme of things which science discloses. It is an anomaly, an exception. Go into any of the popular churches and listen to a sermon on salvation by Jesus Christ. What you hear will be for the most part a meaningless jargon. It does not connect itself with anything else you know in the world. You shall hear something about blood and about sacrifice and about atonement; that is just as much outside of our knowledge as the cabalism of the Jews or the remedies of the Indian medicine man. If the preacher were to say: "My friends, we are all brothers of this man Jesus Christ, flesh of his flesh and bone of his bone; what he felt we may feel; what he saw we may see; what he did we may do; we have in kind, though maybe not in degree, the same power and capacities he had; we can live as pure, as noble, as disinterested a life as he lived; we may show, in a measure, the same meekness, gentleness, humility, unselfishness, lovingness, charity, truthfulness, brotherliness as he showed, and that coming to him means coming to our better selves, to the Jesus within us, to our capacity to be and do like him," we should understand him. He would be speaking words of soberness and truth. If he were to say that salvation by Jesus Christ meant salvation by cultivating Christ-like qualities, not the believing this or that about Christ, but by living up to the Christ-like ideal, — if he were to say these or the like things, his words would be strong by the whole weight of science and of human experience. What he does say or do is to unfold the plan of salvation, that curious device by which the first person of the Trinity cheated the devil of his due, and in which such cabalistic terms as the council of the Godhead, the fall of man, imputed guilt, and vicarious atonement, play the leading parts.

My orthodox brother will charge that I speak as a natural man to whom these things are foolishness. Well, the natural man has come a good way to the front these latter days. He will not be sat down on with impunity any longer. He is backed up as he has never been before. Time was when he was utterly squelched and disposed of by simply telling him that he was the natural man, one with natural forces, with the carnal, unregenerate, devil-beridden natural world, and that all good things were on the side of the extra-natural or theological man. He was a poor, lost, and ruined creature — an outcast in the universe. But how are the tables turned! It is your theological man, your man of miracles and special providences, of witches and demons, of riddles and revelations, who is on the defensive now. He is stripped almost naked; he has barely a foot of ground to stand upon. The natural man, the man of reason, has the whole of science, the enormous sum of human knowledge, the whole visible order of the universe on his side. Our civilization is his, the future is his, the stars in their courses fight for him. We have learned, if we have learned anything, that spirit loves matter, that it blooms out of it, and that it is from within and not from without that salvation comes; that the race of man has many saviours and must have many more. The enigmas of the old theology are exploded; religion takes its place in line with other normal forces, unfolding out of man as surely as his poetry or his art. It is natural or it is nothing. No matter how truly supernatural the devotee may think religion, his very delusion is natural. Those poor wretches who confessed themselves witches during the witch-ridden age were the victims of a natural delusion.

In all religious matters, in fact in all subjective matters, we are fast coming to see that truth is not a fixed quantity that may be seized upon and monopolized by any sect or church. We are beginning to see even further than that. We are beginning to see that there are no distinctively religious truths; that all truth is one; that the faculties that distinguish truth from falsehood in any sphere are always one and the same. Religion is a sentiment, and is true as a sentiment; it is real, but the objects of faith may be real and they may not. They are not truths unless they are verifiable. The world within we re-create daily. The outer world is always the same. It is only our ability to deal with it that fluctuates. Hence the facts of science, so far as they are facts, are constant, while systems of ethics, religions, philosophies, theories of this or that, are in endless mutation. Pilate's question, What is truth? was not the question of a scoffer. What, indeed, is the truth about the melting and changing forms and figures we see in the cloud-land of man's moral and religious experience? Are we not beginning slowly to see that there are not, nor can be, any final truths in these matters, in the sense in which there are final truths in science?

Where religion imitates science and formulates a creed in which it seeks to give permanent intellectual form to its so-called truths, it takes a false step. The creed, as we see, soon pinches and must be made over new. When man draws hard and fast lines in religious matters, he soon finds himself compelled to pull down and build larger. The conception of God is being completely made over in the religious conscience of our time. As man becomes more benevolent and merciful he makes himself a more benevolent and merciful God. The God of our Puritan fathers will not do for us at all. The moral difficulties of Calvinism are getting to be as insurmountable as the intellectual difficulties of Catholicism. The God of to-day, or the divine ideal towards which the religious conscience of our time is struggling, one may feel some liking for, but the God of

145

IX

REASON AND PREDISPOSITION

THAT most men in the formation of their opinions are governed more by predisposition or unconscious bent and tendency than by reason is obvious enough. Indeed, reason is the faculty by which we seek to justify the course of this deeper-seated predetermining force or bent. We gravitate naturally to this opinion or to that, to conservatism or to radicalism, to realism or to idealism, and we seek for reasons that favor *our* course. Considerations that are of great force with certain types of mind are of little or no force with certain other types. Reasons that confirm what we already believe or want to believe, how forcible they are! But if they point the other way, how lightly we esteem them! Reason is like the compass which the sailor takes to sea with him and to which he constantly refers in keeping his course, but which has nothing to do in determining that course. Every man goes his own way, and of the agents that determine him in any given direction, whether original bent, inherited traits, the influence of his training or of his environment, he is but dimly conscious; his reason is the conscious instrument by which he tries to steer on his predetermined way.

Hence it is that Cardinal Newman says that in his going over to Rome it was not logic that carried him on; "as well might one say that the quicksilver in the barometer changes the weather. It is the concrete being that reasons; pass a number of years and I find my mind in a new place; how? The whole man moves; paper logic is but the record of it." The great cardinal may have been logical after he once started for Rome, but what made him drift that way? It was because he was a born papist from the first; one can see the stamp of Rome upon him in his youth.

Probably most of us come into possession of our religious beliefs in the same way Newman did, — we grow into them; they are slowly and unconsciously built up in our minds. We think we reason ourselves into them, but we find ourselves in possession of them, and then we seek to justify our course by an appeal to reason. In our day religious opinion or religious feeling sets less and less store by dogmas and creeds; it no longer goes in the leading-strings of set forms and outward authority. Natural knowledge is in the ascendant. The sun of science has actually risen, indeed rides high up in the heavens, and the things proper to the twilight or half knowledge of a few centuries ago flee away, or are seen to be shadows and illusions. The great mother church may draw her curtains and retrim her lamps and make believe it is still night in the world, but those outside know better, and those inside are bound to find it out by and by. Newman is a careful reasoner, but what would satisfy his mind will not satisfy all, because we are not all going his way. What is a fair breeze to one may be a foul breeze to another.

Newman's reason follows his belief, never leads it. Any number of difficulties, intellectual difficulties, he says, do not make a doubt. Certainly not where experience attests the thing to be true. But suppose it is contrary to all experience, contrary to all the principles upon which human observation is founded, — how then?

Of course we are not always to reject a proposition simply because we cannot understand it or penetrate it with the light of reason. We do not know how or why species vary, but we know they do vary. We do not understand the laws of heredity, but we know heredity to be a fact, and so with thousands of other things. Do we know transubstantiation to be a fact? There are difficulties in the way of evolution, but these difficulties are not such as violate nature, but such as indicate that nature may have taken another course in the production of species. The difficulties in the way of believing in the efficacy of holy water, or that the image of the Madonna winked, or that Elisha made iron swim, are of quite another sort; these assumptions contravene all the rest of our knowledge.

At the best, we all see the truth through a glass, darkly, never face to face. We cannot separate ourselves from our times or our country. We see things through the medium of race, of family, of public opinion, of culture, of books. The Frenchman sees through one medium, the German through another, the Englishman through another, the American another. The Northern races see things differently from the Southern races, the Celt from the Saxon, women from men, youth from age. The impressionable, imaginative man cannot be expected to give the same report of what he sees as the heavy, phlegmatic man. We believe according to our capacity for belief. Scientific considerations have no weight with some minds, — theological considerations have little weight with others. I tried a long time the other day to convince a man that the earth was round and turned round. But I could not. He *knew* better. Equally in vain did I once try to convince a farmer that the pump did not *suck* or draw the water, as he supposed, but that the weight of the outside air did it all. In higher and in less demonstrable matters it is usually equally futile to try to change people's opinions or convictions, at least by a direct attack upon them. Appeal to a man's reason, or to his argumentative faculties, and you have started a game at which two can play. The indirect method is better; aim to beget in him a state of mind, or a way of looking at things, that is incompatible with the belief you seek to remove. This is undermining his opinion.

Outside of mathematics and the exact sciences, what we call reason is a very uncertain matter. In the region of exact demonstration all minds capable of a logical process must reach nearly the same conclusions; but in the region of man's moral, intellectual, and emotional nature, — in politics, in religion, in metaphysics, in taste, — the field is so vast and complicated, there is room for so many disturbing elements to come in, such as temperament, training, personal bias, family, race, imagination, sentiment, the time spirit, that the results of reason are as various as the complexions of men. What is a convincing reason to one man is no reason at all to another. Men draw precisely opposite conclusions from the same premises. I suppose every soul builds for itself, or has built for it, a house of reason in which to dwell. With some it is a very frail structure, and will not bear any pressure at all; with others it is much more massive and strong; but with none is it invulnerable. Some use the material which others reject; but the great mass of us, I suppose, take the houses we find already built; we are not capable of building even the rudest structure for ourselves. But reasons of some sort to put round about us and house us from the great inhospitable out of doors we must have. Most men can give plenty of reasons for their religious and political beliefs. You and I may not accept them, but that does not invalidate them to these particular persons. They afford the shelter the mind craves, and that is enough. Of course there is no final reason in these fields, no one inevitable conclusion, as in mathematics. The clearest and strongest mind brings the clearest and strongest reason. In the purely human sphere all things are relative. The little and the big, the high and the low, the hot and the cold, pleasure and pain, good and bad, right and wrong, true and false, are relative terms; and the best reason is that which covers the most facts, which is the most complete induction. We dispute with each other about the wisdom or expediency of a political measure, but the absolute reason has nothing to say upon either side; the truth or falsity of the matter is relative.

We come by our opinions and beliefs upon most subjects by a slow and obscure process. We think we are guided to them by the light of reason, but as a rule we are not. There is some determining force that goes before reason. This determining force is our idiosyncrasy, natural bent, or predisposition, the pattern to which our souls are cut, and over which we have as little control as over our statures or our temperaments. We are born Calvinists or Methodists or Catholics, or Whigs or Tories. The mind has its natural affinities and repulsions. Its door opens as by a secret spring at the knock of certain truths, and is fast bolted against others to which the next mind again opens. We read arguments in favor of certain views to which we are opposed, and they have no weight with us; our minds do not open to them, or, if they enter for a moment, they are quickly hustled out by other considerations which have the precedence there. We are housed in our opinions, and we resist being turned out of doors and having another and a different roof built over our heads.

I recently read the confessions of a Catholic about his religion. He said he could not accept the Bible upon its own evidence; he must have some exterior authority to authenticate it. This he found in his church. His reason revolted at the idea of an infallible book, but not at the idea of an infallible Pope. He could accept one upon its own evidence, but not the other. Was not this man a born Catholic?

"Few minds in earnest," says Cardinal Newman, "can remain at ease without some sort of rational grounds for their religious belief;" but see what kind of "grounds" he plants his house of faith upon. Most of us would consider them treacherous and shifting sands. Read how he argues himself into accepting the dogma of transubstantiation. "Why should it not be? What's to hinder it? What do I know of substance and matter? Just as much as the greatest philosopher, and that is nothing at all." Certain types of mind will find this reasoning suf-

153

ficient. If we are already convinced, how little it takes to convince us! To certain other types of mind it is very much like reasoning whether or not Santa Claus comes down the chimney. What's to hinder? The chimney is open at the top, and has a definite capacity of good, honest cubic inches. How do I know who or what comes down the chimney, with its open shaft up there in the mysterious darkness? Newman accepts the dogma of the Immaculate Conception on scarcely more tangible grounds; namely, "because it so intimately harmonizes with that circle of recognized dogmatic truths into which it has been recently received." To some minds it would occur to ask, Does it harmonize with the circle of known facts governing human propagation? In reasoning himself into a belief in the infallibility of the Pope, Newman makes a long run before he jumps; he begins with a series of startling assumptions. Suppose this to be true, and that to be true, and still another thing to be true, and then the leap, and the chasm is cleared. But Newman was a born Romanist. He says, " From the age of fifteen dogma has been the fundamental principle of my religion;" "religion as a mere sentiment is to me a dream and a mockery." Religion as a dogma has drenched the world in blood; as a sentiment it has refined and elevated the race. As a dogma it says, "Believe as I do, or I will kill you;" as a sentiment it says, "Except ye become as little children."

REASON AND PREDISPOSITION

Reason never led man to a religion. Religion does not exist for his reason, but for his emotional nature, his fears, his hopes, his spiritual aspirations, and as an escape from the disappointments and the materialism of life. Probably no religion that has yet existed can stand the test of reason — religion, I mean, not as a system of ethics, but as a system of dogma. The question for an outsider to ask concerning the religion of a race or people is not, Is it true? but, Is it elevating? Is it saving? It seems to me that the various lines of reasoning that have been resorted to to prove the truth of Christianity have only weakened its hold upon faith. When men believe without reason, or in defiance of it, then is religion strong and has a career. I can well understand what Cardinal Newman meant when he said, "I do not shrink from uttering my firm conviction that it would be a gain to the country were it vastly more superstitious, more bigoted, more gloomy, more fierce in its religion than at present it shows itself to be." Is not that the Catholic note, though Newman when he uttered it was not yet a Catholic? But it was the spirit of dogmatic religion that spoke there, the fierce cry of the spirit of the earlier centuries when the church moulded the world in its own image, and fire and fagots awaited the man who said to it, "Come, let us reason together." In saying that no religion can stand the test of reason, I mean, of course, the reason of the disbeliever, the reason

cannot, or does not. He starts with the belief, and probably the road by which he came to it is deep down beyond the reach of his consciousness. He says his conviction of the truth of revealed religion and of the authority of the church as its divine guardian and exponent is not due to "emotional feelings and sentiments, and still less to any declarations of authority," but to the "evident dictates of calm and solid reason." Yet these reasons he cannot set forth so as to satisfy Sir James or any other impartial reader. It is evidently his belief in them that convinces him of their truth.

The Catholic note which Mr. Mivart sounds is unmistakable, and is frequently met with in the current British reviews. Here it is in an essay by Aubrey de Vere: "Reason knows her own limits. When the subject matter lies wholly within those limits, as in science, truth is proved by reason; in matters capable of man's apprehension in part, and yet partially beyond those limits, it is proved *to* reason. In the former case Reason asserts; in the latter case she confesses." How plausible this is, and how cleverly it prepares the way for the authority of the Catholic church! It is saying, in effect, that there are certain reasonable things which yet lie outside of the limits of reason, and which reason is to accept without proof. Are there any limits to reason in the sense here implied? I think not. All reasonable things are to be apprehended by the reason alone. Nothing can be proved to reason but by reason. To say that a reasonable proposition is first apprehended by some faculty besides reason and then brought home to the latter, is like saying that a visible object can be seen by something other than the eye. Microscopes and telescopes aid the eye by multiplying and extending its powers in its own direction; not by the addition of any new principle of vision. In the same way the discovery of the law of gravitation or the laws of Kepler arms and extends the human reason, of which they are the fruit. Power alone can use power, the eye alone can use the telescope, not the hand or the ear. There are realities of the material world which the eye does not acquaint us with, as sound and odor, for instance, but in its own sphere the eye is not barred, and in its own sphere the reason is not limited. True, there are many things which it cannot penetrate — this nearest of all facts, for instance, how we live and move and have our being; neither can any other faculty penetrate the mystery. It is not reason that sees the truth of poetry or art; the most reasonable man in the world may fail to see the poetic or artistic truth of Homer or Angelo. Neither is it reason that sees the truth of religion, using the word in its largest sense, as dissociated from all creeds; no, it is the soul, the higher intelligence, that sees the truth or the worth of these things. But it is the reason that sees the truth or falsity of the dogmas of the church,

158

the science of it, its theology. These are propositions addressed to the understanding and not to the soul. It is reason that grasps the philosophy of literature and art, but literature and art themselves address quite a different part of our nature. In its own spheres we must give reason its way. In the objective world of fact and experience we have no guide but reason. How far reason can deal with the inner subjective world is another matter. "The kingdom of heaven cometh not with observation," nor with reasoning. Logic may deepen a man's religious convictions, but it is doubtful if it can ever produce them in the first place. Something more personal and emotional is necessary. I should say that it was not even necessary that a religion be true to the reason to save men, at least in this world; it is necessary that it be true to the moral sense — that is, that it be worthy, that it cherish a higher ideal. Calvinism had long outraged men's reason, but it got along very well till it began to impinge upon their moral sense, their sense of justice, of mercy, of fitness. Reason can be silenced, but "infant damnation" arouses something that will not, at this age of the world, be silenced. The ideal of Calvinism is beginning to topple, and when this is the case with a creed its power for good is gone.

This, then, seems to be the truth with regard to reason: —

It is the lamp by which our feet are guided, but

X

RELIGIOUS TRUTH

WHEN hard pressed, theological writers often take refuge in the statement that there is some kind of evidence that is superior to scientific evidence in matters that pertain to objects of sense and experience. Thus Dr. Temple, in his Bampton Lectures on the "Relations between Religion and Science," says in behalf of miracles, that if the student of science is to admit a breach in the uniformity of nature, "it can only be by stepping outside of his science for the time and conceiving the possibility that there is some other truth beside scientific truth, and some other kind of evidence beside scientific evidence." Unless he does this, he is in a groove, and is like "the student who when he first saw a locomotive engine looked perseveringly for the horses that impelled it, because he had never known, and consequently could not imagine, any other mode of producing such motion." But if the student did persevere, he surely found the horses at last, a real tangible force that propelled the engine, and one that worked according to uniform law. For my part, I confess I cannot conceive of any evidence that can be brought in support of miracles that shall not be in its nature scientific, that is, addressed to our rational faculties. What is this other evidence to which Dr. Temple alludes? He would probably say it is the evidence that a higher will interferes and sets aside or reverses the ordinary processes of nature; but do we not want evidence that a higher will does so interfere, and must not this evidence be scientific? that is, adequate to convince the mind? We can admit a breach in the uniformity of nature only upon the same *kind* of evidence as that which leads us to deny the breach; that is, evidence that appeals to reason and experience. It must be tangible, objective evidence, and not a theory or a groundless postulate. What proves the interference of this higher will? The miracle. But what proves the miracle? The theory of the higher will.

If there are other truths than scientific truths, and other grounds of certitude than those apprehended by the reason, they are not such as are available when natural law is on trial.

If we ask of a thing, or a measure, or a course of conduct, Is it good or bad, right or wrong? we appeal to the moral sense; if we ask of a thing, Is it beautiful? we appeal to the æsthetic sense. If we ask of a statement or alleged occurrence, Is it true? we appeal to the intellectual sense, to the reason and judgment. And there is no other court but this that can settle the truth or falsity of a propois enough. But the man of science asks, Are they true, not as poetry or fable, but as history? That feeling or mental disposition that responds to fables and allegories is as genuine as that which enables us to detect truth from falsehood, only it cannot take its place; it belongs to a different sphere. There is something in us that delights in fables and in heroic deeds; that rises superior to times and circumstances, and makes the devotion of martyrs and the triumphs of the Davids over the Goliaths tonic and refreshing. There are books and poems that ventilate and tone up a man's whole nature. We are by no means summed up by our knowing faculties. Truth of fact and truth of sentiment make up life, and about in the proportion of the bone and the fleshy tissue in our systems. We may say there is relative truth and absolute truth. All scientific truth if it be truth is absolute; it is verifiable, and must hold good at all times and places. A man's opinion of a matter, that is, his inference from observed facts, is true from his conditions and point of view; it is the outcome of his relations, capacity, and antecedents; it is modified by his temperament, his culture, his health, his sympathies, his race, his environment, and many other things. If, strictly speaking, there are religious truths, truths that in no wise depend upon your view or my view of the case, they are verifiable. But religious truths I should say are relative truths, and any attempt to make them fixed and absolute, as the creedmongers have tried to do, must end in failure. Truth in all subjective matters is not a fixed quantity; it is something that must be ever newly grown like organic Nature herself.

A recent theological writer says that when men accustomed to the demonstrative evidence of science "enter a province where moral evidence rather than demonstration prevails, they are not unnaturally inclined to suppose that nothing in it is settled, nothing ascertained," and very reasonably, I think. Nothing can be *settled* except upon demonstrative evidence; you may think it settled and wake up next day to find that the floods of new inquiry have come and set it all afloat again. Moral evidence can settle nothing permanently; it may produce conviction in men's minds to-day, which some new thought or new spirit will chafe under to-morrow. The moral evidences of Christianity — its wonderful growth from such obscure beginnings, the noble lives it has inspired, its power for good in the world — have great weight, but they do not settle the questions that vex us. Other religions have grown in the same way, and been the inspiration of heroic lives and the bond of national prosperity. It will not do to say, as is so often said, that the European nations owe all to Christianity; what Christianity owes to the quality and spirit of the European races remains to be determined. Why did it not transform the

Eastern peoples as well? Science has done more for the development of Western civilization in one hundred years than Christianity did in eighteen hundred. Again, why has science not done as much for the Oriental nations? There we are; to dogmatize in these matters is dangerous business. The factor of race, the factor of environment, climate, geology, rivers, mountain chains, variety of coast line, etc., all enter into the problem.

The writer I have already quoted says, "Too high demands cannot be made on theology as to the legitimacy and scientific accuracy of its methods." The scientific method is the same whether in the hands of the man of science or the theologian. It is simply proving all things and holding fast that which is true.

When our doctors of divinity treat Christianity as an evolution, do they not thereby abandon the claim that it is a revelation? It cannot be both. If it is an evolution, if it came logically and naturally out of what went before, if it was a growth, a development of the religious conscience of man, then it takes its place in the course of historical events, and the man of science may accept it. In that case, what becomes of the claim that it was a revelation, something that had no relation to what went before, something interjected into the course of mundane history from without, an interpolation, a miraculous ray of light from out the heavens? Science knows evolution, but it can make nothing of revelation. Pilate's old question, What is truth? is never out of date.

Ask what is the truth in mathematics, and the answer is easy: two and two make four; a straight line is the shortest distance between two points; the angles of a triangle are equal to two right angles, etc. Ask what is the truth in science, and the answer comes as promptly, though here the field is as yet only fairly entered upon; ask what is the truth in politics, and here we are bound to say all men are liars; the truth is whatever you can convince yourself is true. Ask what is the truth in political economy, in ethics, in metaphysics, and lastly in religion, and the answers are as various as the minds of men. It is certain that it is not a fixed quantity, that it is relative, and changes as the wants and conditions of men change. We cannot close our minds upon the truth in these spheres and say " I have it," any more than we can close our hands upon the light and say " I have it." The good and the bad, the beautiful and the ugly, are relative terms; no fast and hard lines can here be drawn, all is plastic, fluctuating, growing. But science draws fast and hard lines and can alone formulate definite truths. A friend and correspondent of Coleridge, writing for the benefit of his children, said that through the influence of that philosopher he had been able to arrive at settled and definite conclusions upon all

167

matters to which he attached value or interest. And then he adds with great wisdom, "When I say that I have arrived at settled conclusions, you will not for a moment believe that my opinions can or *ought* to be received by others of a totally different experience as *truths* for their minds; still less that matters which depend upon individual experience and temperament can be permanent truths for all time." What a lesson for us all. Every man builds or tries to build himself a house of truth of some sort, to shelter him from the great void, but how foolish to expect us all to build alike or go to the same quarry for our material; or that our house could serve for our children for all coming time. How long it will serve depends upon how large, how well, how conveniently it is built.

Spiritual truths are spiritually discerned undoubtedly, but I should deny that the content of the popular creeds belonged to the region of spiritual truths. They contain definite propositions that relate to historical events, — to the soul of man considered as an entity in and of itself, to its nature and destiny. They make definite statements about the actual world of events, about an historical personage, about a concrete book, about a past race of men, about birth and generation. Now these are not spiritual truths, and they are not spiritually discerned. They are material truths, if truths at all, and they are discerned by the reason and understanding. What, then, is spiritual truth? That which appeals to the soul as distinct from the reason and the intellect, or to our higher and finer sense of the beauty and mystery of the world. The Sermon on the Mount contains spiritual truth: The kingdom of heaven is within you; except ye become as little children; unto the pure are all things pure. The brotherhood of man is a spiritual truth. St. Paul is full of spiritual truth. Emerson's essays are full of spiritual truth, as are all the great poems of the world.

We want the exact scientific truth in many things, — in all that concerns our physical relation to the world, in all the practical affairs of life, in agriculture, in mechanics, in political economy, in all that pertains to trade, to money, to banking, and to currency. The Occidental mind wants this same kind of truth in its religion because its religion is a definite means to a definite end; it is in a way a question of climate and subsistence; it has reference entirely to well-being in some future state. If there is no immortality, we have no use for religion. If a man die, shall he live again? Is there a God as literally as there is a governor or a president? Is the Bible the word of God? Did Christ rise from the dead? Is the church the gate to heaven? If so, which church? In the popular mind religion hinges upon these questions, and it demands a scientific answer to them. The good Catholic believes the Pope to be as actually and literally the deputy or vicegerent of God as the priest is the visible servant of the Pope.

Into the formation of our minds and into the conduct of our lives there enter truths, opinions, and sentiments. Four fifths of our lives are probably made up of sentiment; that is, feeling, aspiration, attraction, repulsion. A sentiment may be relatively true or false, it may arise from a narrow view or a broad view, but it is equally potent whether true or false. Demonstrable truth enters into our lives scarcely more than the mineral elements enter into our bodies, but our lives could not go on for a moment without them.

The religious emotion is true as an emotion; it is when we try to translate it into the language of the reason and the understanding that the trouble begins. Its reality does not prove the reality of the definite objects upon which it centres in our case any more than it did with the pagan peoples. If religion is not its own reward as much as art or science is, if it is not salvation here and now, if it be not in the life and character of a man like Ingersoll as truly as in the life and character of a man like Mr. Moody, then it is a delusion and a snare.

XI

POINTS OF VIEW

WHAT a wide difference it makes whether we look upon the world from the point of view of art, the point of view of science or the intellect, or from the point of view of evangelical religion. Only from the latter point of view do we see what is called sin. The theologian looks upon the world, and he sees wickedness, corruption, sin. The man of intellect looks upon it, and he sees a thousand interesting problems and objects, issues, tendencies, struggles, failures, and fulfillments. The artist looks upon it, and he sees pictures everywhere, form and proportion, light and shade, colors and values. How unartistic is the heaven of the theologian to the artist; how uninteresting and impossible to the man of science. You cannot make a picture all white; you cannot have power and motion, growth and development, in a world where there is no clashing or opposition or imperfection, where there is no evil, but only the good of the pious enthusiast.

To the scientist and to the artist or poet, the world as we know it is a much more desirable place to

live in than the world as imagined and longed for
by the devout of Christendom. Without sin in the
world, where would be the merit of the saint? Without hindrance and delays and disappointments how
could character be· developed? Indeed, what a
blank, meaningless world this would be if the principles of good and evil were not continually wres-
tling with each other in it. This is the verdict of the
intellect and the æsthetic faculties, and this is the
fruit of the forbidden tree. We are not to know this,
lest our struggle with evil be relaxed. There is no
doubt need enough of the preacher to warn us of
our dangers, and to hold up before us the standard
of the absolute good.

Still, Christendom has not yet succeeded in making
its heaven attractive; that is, attractive to the intellect, or to the faculties that find their fulfillment in
this world. We have to imagine ourselves differently
constituted beings to see any joy in it; not merely
beings of a higher spiritual capacity, but beings fundamentally different. The gods of the ancient world,
the pagan gods, were more or less attractive; there
was much in them that the natural man responded
to. But the God of Christendom, the Jehovah of the
Jews, or the Almighty Despot of Calvinism, is not
attractive; we do not spontaneously like him; Jesus
as portrayed in the Gospels is attractive or lovable,
but as interpreted in the old theology he is not attractive. But our good brother says, "You must be

changed." Certainly, but this is just what the intellect in the natural man does not want to be. He wants to look at and to understand and appreciate these things from the same point of view from which he regards and appreciates nature, life, the visible universe. The man is not changed when he becomes a poet; his feelings and capacities are heightened. He is not changed when he becomes a philosopher; his mind is deepened and enlarged. But to become a Christian, as our fathers understood it, he is to be radically broken up and turned about as St. Paul was. His point of view is shifted to another sphere. His interest is entirely transferred to another state of existence. To the Christian this is a lost and ruined world, the races of men are all on the road to perdition, the heathen nations have fed the fires of hell in all ages, this life is but ashes and dung. For the intellect or the natural man to sympathize with this view would be to negative and discredit its own powers and aims.

One of the first difficulties the man of science has with Christianity is that it is not commensurate with the race or with history. What are you going to do, he asks, with the splendid peoples that lived before the time of Christ? As a phase of man's religious growth and culture he can understand it, but as a system that excludes from all possibilities of salvation the greater part of the human race, he is bound to repudiate it. Christianity affords the highest religious type. This is reasonable; that it inaugurated the only possible salvation, this is not reasonable. Our fathers got along without steam and electricity, and found life tolerable. Greece flourished before Christ and achieved splendid results. Christianity is a great advance, but it is no more the beginning of man's spiritual life than Buddhism or any other pagan religion was. All this is from the point of view of the impartial intellect, and is this point of view to be denied?

To the intellectual man evil is only the privation of good as cold is the privation of heat. Indeed, this is what Saint Augustine, speaking as a philosopher, said. As the life of the globe depends upon degrees of heat and cold, depends upon differences, fluctuations, inequalities, so human development depends upon a mixture of good and evil. Overcome evil with good, that is growth in morals; overcome ignorance with knowledge, that is growth in intellect. Sin as a state of condemnation or alienation from God, in consequence of Adam's transgression, — of this theological conception of sin, what can the intellect know? It can know nothing. It sees that the condition of life everywhere is struggle, in the vegetable as well as in the animal world, in the spiritual as in the intellectual realm. It sees that the law of the survival of the fittest is everywhere operative. It sees that ideal good never is and never can be attained. The ideal is an air line;

the practical is the devious path through bog and over hill.

Wherever man is, the ideal will soar above him. Wherever man is, pain and conflict will attend him. One of our poets, Mr. Gilder, has dared affirm that wherever God is, are pain and struggle also.

" By all most noble in us, by the light that streams
Into our waking dreams,
    Ah! we who know what Life is, let us live!
Clearer and freer who shall doubt?
Something of dust and darkness cast forever out;
But Life, still Life, that leads to higher Life.—
Even though the highest be not free from the immortal
       strife."

.   .   .   .

" For in all worlds there is no Life without a pang, and
       can be naught."

From the point of view of art and science, the unconverted heathen is a more interesting creature than the converted. Our knowledge of this world tells us that the religion and civilization of a higher race cannot be thrust upon a lower. Every people must work out its own salvation, must come to its religion by an original experience of its own. But the missionary, with his eye upon the other world, sees these pagan races in imminent danger of some terrible *post-mortem* calamity, and he fancies he has the means to rescue them from it.

Our religious teachers have always admitted the intellectual difficulties in the way of their faith; the older ones have declared them unsurmountable. The intellect knows nothing of a revealed religion, of vicarious atonement and the like. All these things, all the supernatural elements in our faith, have their origin and authority in the religious sentiment, in the hopes, fears, intuitions, and aspirations of mankind. Whatever proof these afford, it is a kind of proof that cannot be addressed to our rational faculties.

The mere intellectual assent to a religious doctrine or scheme is usually barren, because religion has reference to action, conduct, life. The will, the heart, the imagination, must be enlisted, the moral nature aroused. It is doubtful if the great mass of mankind give any intellectual assent to the doctrines of their faith. The fathers of the church, in attempting to give an intellectual basis to them, were led into curious absurdities. Thus Irenæus said there must be four Gospels, instead of three, because there were four winds, and four corners of heaven. Our theologians, in their appeal to reason, have not fared much better. Worship, veneration, adoration, are not intellectual acts, but motions of the spirit. Our assent to a doctrine of science, on the other hand, is necessarily intellectual. It is not barren, because intellectual results are alone to be expected. The doctrine of evolution has stimulated the mind of our

age to an unprecedented degree. It has a bearing
upon religion only when religion appeals to the reason with a rival scheme of creation. Science alone
can meet our demand for knowledge of the visible
world. But after science has done its best, is not
the mystery as deep as ever? Is there not the same
ground for faith, worship, adoration, as ever?

Religion is older than science. Man worshiped
and adored long before he sought the reasons and
the meaning of things. At the same time it must be
owned that man has become less and less religious
from the first dawn of civilization to the present
day. The intellectual point of view has prevailed
more and more. With all our Christianity, the
ancient communities, Egypt, Greece, Rome, were
much more religious than we are; that is, life, both
individual and natural, faced much more toward
the unseen supernatural powers. Indeed, the natural did hardly exist; the supernatural was all in
all. The gods played the leading part in their his-
tories; they really play no part at all in ours. Once a
year our chief magistrate issues his formal Thanks-
giving Proclamation, and the people through-
out the length and breadth of the land fall to and
gorge themselves with roast turkey; this is our religious rite as a nation. With the ancient pagan peoples, religious motives entered into every act. Renan
does not exaggerate when he says that the "religion
of the ancients was the spinal marrow of the nation

itself." At Platæa both the Greeks and the Persians refrained for ten days from making the attack, because the oracles and the victims were unfavorable. The armies had their diviners, upon whose word the generals waited. Not military considerations, but religious omens determined them when to strike. No expedition was undertaken without consulting the oracles, and no action fought without offering sacrifice. All through the Middle Ages, see what a part religion, or what we now call superstition, played in the world!

With the ancient peoples religion bore no essential relation to morality ; the most dark and revolting crimes were committed in the name of the gods. The great change in the modern world is that there is no religion without morality. This is the law for individuals. Nations are probably as immoral to-day as ever they were, just as selfish and revengeful.

The intellectual point of view is bound to prevail more and more. Our knowing faculties are certainly outstripping our intuitions and our devotional instincts. What will be the final result ?

The current religion gets into trouble the moment it would make its point of view coincide with the intellectual point of view, because its view is partial and personal ; it seeks a particular good, while the intellect seeks all truth, seeks to see the thing as it is in itself. Religion seeks to see the thing only as it stands related to its particular end, helping or hindering. The man who is concerned about the safety of his soul sustains quite a different relation to the world from the man who is concerned only about what is true, or what is beautiful, or what is good, in and of themselves. Only the latter is a disinterested observer.

Will religion survive science? Not as dogma and creed, or as intellectual propositions, or belief in the supernatural, but as spiritual attraction, as faith, hope, love. When man ceases to feel, in some measure, the mystery and spirituality of the universe, and the presence of a power in which we live, and move, and have our being, he will have reversed his history and gone backward instead of forward.

XII

GOD AND NATURE

HALF a century or more ago a pious Scotch family lately come to this country moved into the town where I was born. As they were coming through a deep gorge in the mountains where the scenery was unusually wild and forbidding, one of the little boys, looking forth upon the savage and desolate prospect, nestled closer to his mother and asked with bated breath, "Mither, is there a God here?" The little boy's question sprang from a feeling which probably most of us share. The desolate, the terrible, the elemental, the inhuman in nature, are always more or less a shock to one's notions of the existence of a beneficent Supreme Being. In storms at sea, amid the fury and wild careering of the elements, or in tempest and darkness upon the land, when riot and destruction stalk abroad, how faint and far off seems the notion of the fatherhood of God! The other day, in looking over some of Professor Langley's views of the sun, photographic representations of those immense craters or openings into the solar furnace into which our little earth would disappear as quickly as a snowflake into the

181

mouth of a blast furnace, the question of the little Scotch boy came to me, "Is there a God here?" It is incredible. The utmost one can do, he cannot begin to conceive of a being adequate to these things. Under the old dispensation, before the advent of science, when this little world was all, and the sun, moon, and stars were merely fixtures overhead to give light and warmth, the conception of a being adequate to create and control it all was easier. The storms were expressive of his displeasure, the heavens were his throne, and the earth was his footstool. But in the light of modern astronomy, one finds himself looking in vain for the God of his fathers, the magnified man who ruled the ancient world. In his place we have an infinite and eternal Power whose expression is the visible universe, and to whom man is no more and no less than any other creature.

Hence when the man of science says, "There is no God," he only gives voice to the feeling of the inadequacy of the old anthropomorphic conception, in the presence of the astounding facts of the universe.

When I look up at the starry heavens at night and reflect upon what it is that I really see there, I am constrained to say, "There is no God." The mind staggers in its attempt to grasp the idea of a being that could do that. It is futile to attempt it. It is not the works of some God that I see there. I am face to face with a power that baffles speech. I see no lineaments of personality, no human traits, but an energy upon whose currents solar systems are but bubbles. In the presence of it man and the race of man are less than motes in the air. I doubt if any mind can expand its conception of God sufficiently to meet the astounding disclosures of modern science. It is easier to say there is no God. The universe is so *un*human, that is, it goes its way with so little thought of man. He is but an incident, not an end. We must adjust our notions to the discovery that things are not shaped to him, but that he is shaped to them. The air was not made for his lungs, but he has lungs because there is air; the light was not created for his eye, but he has eyes because there is light. All the forces of nature are going their own way; man avails himself of them, or catches a ride as best he can. If he keeps his seat, he prospers; if he misses his hold and falls, he is crushed. Mankind used to think that the dews and rains were sent for their benefit, and the church still encourages this idea by praying for rain in times of drought, but the notion is nearly dissipated. To such a mind as Cardinal Newman the spectacle of the world caused a similar moral shiver and doubt to that which crossed the mind of the little Scotch boy when he looked out upon the wild pass in the mountains. He does not see God there; he says it is like looking into a mirror and not seeing his own face. And the proofs that are drawn from without, from the facts of hu-

sions they have found the material for their deities near at hand.

As man arrives at consciousness, he soon recognizes a Power greater than himself, over which he has no control, and of which he is either an object of sport or solicitude. This power is what we call Nature, the nearest and greatest fact of all. This is the mountain of which, or some fragment of which, all peoples have carved their gods, giving them the form and likeness of such ideal as they were capable of.

At first man deifies and worships various objects of visible material nature. The first god was probably the sun. Nearly all early races have been sun worshipers. The splendor, the power, the bounty of the sun is the most obvious of all the facts of nature. Later, as man developed and his mind opened, he made himself gods out of invisible nature. He projected his own ideal into the universe and worshiped that.

Undoubtedly the most skillful artists in this field, as in so many others, were the Greeks; their gods were the most beautiful and interesting of all. Apollo stands as a type of grace and power to all succeeding races. Then their lesser divinities, — how charming, how interesting they all are, the works of master hands.

The old Hebrews were much less as artists, but much greater as prophets; hence Jehovah, the God of the Hebrew Scriptures, is the most awful, the most imposing, and the most imminent of all the gods. How cruel, how terrible, how jealous, — a magnified and heaven-filling despot and king. With a gentle and loving *alter ego* or deputy, who stands between his stern and awful majesty and guilty and trembling man, namely, Jesus Christ, he is still the God of the most enlightened of the human race. With what power and solemnity he figures in the old Bible; how he filled and shook the hearts of the old bards and prophets! Open the Scriptures almost anywhere, and one seems to hear his awful voice, and feel his terrible tread. It shakes the earth; it fills the heavens; the universe is the theatre of his love and wrath. What an abysmal depth of conscience in those old Hebrews; what capacity for remorse, for reverence, for fear, for terror, for adoration; what a sense of the value of righteousness, and of the dreadfulness of sin! In them we see the unsounded depths of the religious spirit, — its tidal seas; bitter and estranging, but sublime. As I have elsewhere said, all other sacred books are tame, are but inland seas, so to speak, compared with this briny deep of the Hebrew Bible. Little wonder it still sways the hearts and lives of men. Their imaginations go out upon it. Immensity broods over it. It is as tender as a tear or as cruel as death. It is a record of the darkest deeds, and luminous with the sublimest devotion and piety.

186

It is archetypal, elemental. The light of eternity is upon its face. Other books, other bibles, are as if written in houses or temples or sheltered groves; here is the solemnity and grandeur of the mountain-tops, or of the great Asiatic plains under the midnight stars. Man is alone with the Eternal, and with fear and trembling walks and talks with him.

How our fathers read and communed with this book! How much of the culture of the world has come out of it! The light, the entertainment, the stimulus, which we find in literature, in art, in science, our fathers found in this volume.

The mystery of life deepens when we set up a being, no matter how large and all powerful, over the universe apart from and independent of it, and to whom we assign human motives and purposes, — some sort of economic scheme with reference to it. When a good man dies with his work half done, how mysterious, we say, that the master of the vineyard should thus strike down one of his most useful servants and spare so many worthless and worse than worthless ones. The universe viewed in the light of anything like human economy is indeed a puzzle. But this is not the right view. We must get rid of the great moral governor, or head director. He is a fiction of our own brains. We must recognize only Nature, the All; call it God if we will, but divest it of all anthropological conceptions. Nature we know; we are of it; we are in it. But this paternal

Providence above Nature, — events are constantly knocking it down. Here is this vast congeries of vital forces which we call Nature, regardless of time because it has all time, regardless of waste because it is the All, regardless of space because it is infinite, regardless of man because man is a part of it, regardless of life because it is the sum total of life, gaining what it spends, conserving what it destroys, always young, always old, reconciling all contradictions, — the sum and synthesis of all powers and qualities, infinite and incomprehensible. This is all the God we can know, and this we cannot help but know. We want no evidence of this God

> " Far or forgot to me is near;
>   Shadow and sunlight are the same;
>   The vanished gods to me appear;
>   And one to me are shame and fame."

Men labor to prove the existence of their God, but labor never so much, and you cannot prove the non-existence of this God. Your proof to the contrary, he is that also.

Such a notion seems to orphan the universe to some souls, but need it be so? This vital Nature out of which we came, out of which father and mother came, out of which all men came, and to which again we all in due time return, why should we fear it or distrust it? It makes our hearts beat and our brains think. When it stops the beating and the thinking, will it not be well also? It looked after us before we were born; it will look after us when we are dead. Every particle of us will be taken care of; the force of every heart-beat is conserved somewhere, somehow. The psychic force or principle of which I am a manifestation will still go on. There is no stoppage and no waste, forever and ever. My consciousness ceases as a flame ceases, but that which made my consciousness does not cease. What comfort is that to the me? Ah, the *me* wants to go on and on. But let the me learn that only Nature goes on and on, that the law which makes the me and unmakes it is alone immortal, and that it is best so. Identity is a thought, a concept of our minds, and not a property of our minds.

The universe is so stupendous, so unspeakable, that we dare not, cannot, name any end or purpose for which it exists. It is because it is. If man exists on other worlds, or if he does not exist, it is all the same. The superior and the inferior planets may run their course and life not appear upon them. It is just like the prodigality, the indifference of Nature. If the conditions are favorable, man will appear; if not, not. They are no more there for his sake than yonder river is there for the sake of the fishes, or yonder clay-bank for the sake of the brickmakers. Space is no doubt strewn with dead worlds and dead suns as thickly as yonder field with dead boulders, and with worlds upon which only the

the fog as any of them." These Dunkers were indeed
wise in their day and generation, and Franklin
himself was perhaps as little in the fog engendered
by narrowness and dogmatism as any man of his
times. If there is one thing certain in the history
of mankind, it is that sects do outgrow their creeds
and are compelled to pull down and build larger
or else be terribly pinched for room. Probably every
one of the evangelical churches is to-day more or
less pinched by its confessions of faith. No one
can read the recent debate of the Congregational
ministers (1886) at Des Moines, on the subject
of Foreign Missions, Future Probation, etc., without seeing how keenly the finer and more expansive
spirit among them felt the hard limitations of their
creed. The Andover professors have tried to enlarge
the creed a little, or rather, they have tried to stretch
it so as to make it less galling to the modern human-
itarian feeling, and for this they are now arraigned,
and by many of their brethren already condemned.
What pagans and heathens most of us still are in
opinion, hardly yet more than half liberated from
the most groveling and materialistic superstitions
of the pre-Christian world! With our creedmakers,
heaven is still a place, hell is still an infernal abode,
God is still a Moloch or a Baal, Christ is still the
victim sacrificed upon the altar to conciliate an
offended deity, religion is still a doctrine and a ceremony, man is still the sport of capricious and super-

Benjamin Franklin

human powers; justice is still reprisal and reversal; and the day of judgment is still an assizes adjourned to some future time. Creeds in our day harden the heart; they shock our religious sensibilities; they make atheists and scoffers.

In a city near me there is a large cemetery, in a neglected corner of which is a multitude of children's graves which have the appearance of being outcasts, reprobates; and so they are. These children were not baptized, therefore they cannot be buried in consecrated ground; their blameless little souls are in hell, and their bodies are huddled together here in this neglected corner. This is a glimpse of the beauty of the Catholic creed. The Jewish cabalists used to believe that the utterance of certain magical words engraved upon the seal of Solomon would transform a man into a brute, or a brute into a man. The Catholics ascribe the same magical power to water in the hands of a priest. When the service is read and the unconscious infant is baptized, at that moment a miraculous change is wrought in its nature, and Rome says with true Christian charity, "Let him be accursed" who believes it not. The mere knowledge of such things is hurtful. And it requires rare Christian forbearance to read the Andover creed and not fall from the grace of brotherly love. Is it not easy to see what short work Jesus would have made of these creedmongers, — he who was the friend of publicans and sinners, the rebuker

193

of formalists, the contemner of lip service, who laid all the emphasis upon the condition of the heart and the attitude of the spirit, who said to the chief priest of the popular religion of his time, "The publicans and harlots go into the kingdom of heaven before you"?

Our doctors of divinity talk glibly of the growth of religious thought, but seem to lose sight of the fact that growth of religious thought means more or less a decay of old beliefs. There is no growth in anything without a casting off and a leaving of something behind. Growth in science is to a great extent the discovery of new facts and principles, which render the old theories and conclusions untenable. See how much we have had to unlearn and leave behind us by reason of Darwin's labors; and further advances already lessen the significance of some of his principles.

But it may be said that religion has not to do with outward facts and laws like science, but with inward spiritual conditions. Then why seek to embody its final truths in formal propositions as if they were matters of exact demonstration like science? The creeds treat religion as objective fact, something to be proved to the understanding and to be lodged in a system of belief, like any of the teachings of physical science. Regarded as such, it is always exposed to the inquiry, Is it true? Is it final? If it is a subjective condition, if the kingdom of heaven is really within, as Christ taught, then the expression of it in outward forms of belief and creed must change as much as any other philosophy or metaphysics change. A noble sentiment mankind will doubtless always admire; a heroic act, self-sacrifice, magnanimity, courage, enthusiasm, patriotism, will always awaken a quick response; so will religion as devotion, or piety, or love, or as an aspiration after the highest good. But as an intellectual conception of God and of the manner of his dealings with man, it must be subject to change and revision like all other intellectual conceptions. Where actual verification cannot take place, as in science or mathematics, belief must forever fluctuate like the forms and colors of summer clouds. The subject of it may always be the same, — God, the soul, the eternal life, — but the relation of these and their final meanings can never be once and forever settled. Theology is at best only a tentative kind of science. Its conclusions cannot have anything like the certitude of scientific truth, because they are not capable of verification.

Principal Tulloch, in his "Movements of Religious Thought in Britain," had the courage to say that "the idea that theology is a fixed science, with hard and fast propositions, partaking of the nature of infallibility, is a superstition which cannot face the light of modern criticism." Tulloch further indicates that the true rational standpoint as to creeds and formulas is a profound distrust of them as professing "to sum up Divine Truth. Useful as 'aids to faith,' they are intolerable as limitations of faith." And "limitations of faith" most of the creeds undoubtedly are.

But the drift of religious feeling, if not of religious opinion, is undoubtedly away from them. Our churches wisely keep their creeds pretty well in the background. When has any one heard a doctrinal sermon? The creeds have been retired to the rear because they are no longer available in front. The world no longer asks what a man believes, but what *is* he? What is his intrinsic worth as a man? Is he capable of honesty, of sobriety, of manliness? Vital original qualities, and not speculative opinions, are certainly what tell most in this world, however it may be in the next.

Religion as a sentiment is strong in these times, but religion as a dogma is weak. The growing disbelief of which we hear so much is a disbelief in the infallibility of dogma, not a disbelief in the need of godliness, purity, spirituality, and noble, disinterested lives. These things move us as much or more than ever, but in the creeds we hear only the rattling of dry bones. How had the Puritan theology been sloughed off by Emerson, and yet what a pure, stimulating, ennobling, religious spirit shone in that man and still shines in his works, — the "saving grace" of heroic thought and aspiration, if they ever existed. The same might be said of Carlyle, rejecter as he was of the creed of his fathers. "Religion cannot be incarnated and settled once for all in forms of creed and worship. It is a continual growth in every living heart — a new light to every seeing eye. Past theologies did their best to interpret the laws under which man was living, and to help him regulate his life thereby. But the laws of God are before us always, whether promulgated in Sinai thunder or otherwise."

The progress of religious thought that has been made in the last half century is indicated in the writings and sermons of such men as Maurice, Campbell, Erskine, Kingsley, Stanley, Arnold, Robertson, Tulloch, Maudsley, and others in Great Britain, and in those of Emerson, Parker, Hedge, and Mulford, in this country, — a progress from the bondage of the letter of the law into the freedom of the spirit. When we think of what these men have said and done, we may look forward with some confidence, as Goethe did, to a time when "all of us by degrees will learn to elevate ourselves out of a Christianity of catechisms and creeds into a Christianity of pure sentiment and noble action."

magnifies the individual into the universal. The "London Spectator," in replying to Frederic Harrison, who thinks the Christian faith could not possibly have originated in an age that had a heliocentric astronomy, sets forth and enforces the opinion that our astronomical science has not in any vital respect altered or impaired the validity of the theological conceptions of the Jewish and Christian revelations. The "Spectator" fails to see that the Semitic dramaturgy sprang out of the colossal egotism of the early races, the races who considered themselves as the special centre and object of creations, — an egotism that science tends directly to overthrow. It is true the old prophets and biblical writers sought to humble and belittle man in the presence of the hosts of the starry heavens, but this was only a momentary reaction from their gigantic egotism, which made Jehovah so solicitous about his chosen people. But this is not the point.

The point is that the Copernican system of astronomy gives us a conception of the order and harmony of the universe and of the *physical* insignificance of our planet and its subordination to other bodies that is utterly inconsistent with our Semitic theology. The two are not homogeneous; they spring from entirely different standpoints. The Israelites may have been God's chosen people, and this earth of ours may be the apple of his eye among the worlds, but the tendency of the study of science is to utterly uproot such notions. Science liberalizes and impersonalizes. To the impartial student of history all peoples are God's people, and all worlds alike the scenes of his power. In the light of modern astronomy what becomes of the notion that the heavens are above us, far away, and are of a higher and purer creation, or hell beneath us, that the earth is corrupted or blighted by the fall, — kindred notions of one theology? Do we not know that the earth is a star in the heavens, as incorruptible and undefiled as the rest? and that all worlds are kindred and of our stuff, that there is no up and no down, no high and no low in the universe? The lightning does not come out of heaven, nor the rain out of heaven, but out of the clouds. An eclipse is not a warning or a calamity, but purely a natural event, merely the lunar or the terrestrial shadow. Our actual physical smallness and insignificance is what science reveals; our grandeur and importance is what the eye and the untutored mind behold.

Science is impersonal; it tends to belittle and diffuse man. Theology and literature tend to exalt him, and concentrate him, and set him above all. Mythology, theology, philosophy, literature, all exaggerate man and distort his true relations to the universe; but in these latter ages comes science and shows man what he really is, where he belongs in the scheme of the whole, and what an insect of an hour, an ephemera of a moment, he really is, and what a bubble is the world he inhabits. In a late religious work by Julia Wedgewood I find this remark: —

"When once Galileo and Newton had forced the world to recognize that Heaven, if it was anywhere, was everywhere, the moral took a new direction. The antithesis of Heaven and Earth vanished from the inward as well as from the outward world. Human nature became interesting for its own sake."

II

One of the most liberal-minded doctors of divinity allowed himself the other day to speak slightingly of the "vaunted scientific method," as if the scientific method was some new-fangled notion that had recently become current, some patent process or labor-saving machine for obtaining truth; as if men had not always used the scientific method; as if it was not as natural to the mind as walking to the body. When we sift evidence or search into the truth or falsity of any objective proposition, we inevitably use the scientific method. It is the method of proceeding from cause to effect, of proving all things, of testing every link in the chain which binds one fact to another. It has come into prominence in our time because of the great advance of physical science. Men are applying this method to questions that heretofore have been considered above its reach. Theological questions are brought within its range, much to the disgust of the theologians. Of many things that have been taken for granted men are beginning to ask, Are they true? and are applying the tests of this kind of truth. All the events and occurrences recorded in the Bible are subject to the inquiry, Are they true? If we apply to them the scientific method, what is the result? James Martineau, for instance, makes use of the scientific method when he shows so convincingly that the Synoptic Gospels must all have been derived from one common source. If these records, he says, were independent accounts of the words and doings of Jesus by the disciples whose names they bear, it is incredible that they should agree so closely in all their details; the different writers would have witnessed and would have recorded different scenes and events. Only of one thirteenth of the days of the public life of Jesus do we have any record in the Synoptic Gospels. Were these Gospels each an original, or the record of independent witnesses, we should have had the events and the utterances of Jesus on more days, since the apostles would not all have been absent and all present at precisely the same time.

The scientific method can no more be ignored or disputed than can the multiplication table. It is as old as the reason of man and is fallible only as man's reason is fallible. It cannot be applied to matters of religious faith, because we here enter a region where proof or verification is not possible.

III

In the ancient temple of Apollo at Delphi lay a stone, the Omphalos, or navel stone, supposed to mark the centre of the earth. And sure enough, it did mark the centre of the earth, though not exactly under the conditions the ancients believed. The ancients supposed the earth had one centre, like a plane or any irregular surface, or as the navel is the centre of the body; but we know now that the earth is a sphere, and that any point upon its surface may serve as its centre. In like manner every religion thinks itself the one final and supreme religion,—thinks itself the centre of the world; and for that race and that people it is the centre of the world; their life, their history, their development, hinges upon it. Our navel stone, Christianity, is the centre of the world for us, and the Buddhist's, the Mohammedan's, is the centre of the world for him. The religion of Apollo was the central fact in the history of Greece. There may be any number of true though opposing and contradictory religions. There may be any number of centres to the infinite. Mathematics, the exact sciences, are always and everywhere the same, but religion is a sentiment, and the forms in which it clothes itself are as various, as changeable, as fleeting, as the forms of summer clouds.

IV

The whole order of the universe favors virtue and is against vice. Things have come to what they are, man has arrived at what he is, the grass and flowers clothe the fields, the trees thrive and bear wholesome fruit, the air is sweet, and water quenches thirst through the action of the same principles by which we see that virtue is good and vice bad. Things have clashed and warred and devoured each other through past eternities, and out of the final adjustment, the balance at which they have at last arrived, we see that virtue is to be sought and vice to be shunned; we see that a good man's life is the fruit of the same balance and proportion as that which makes the fields green and the corn ripen. It is not by some fortuitous circumstance, the especial favor of some god, but by living in harmony with immutable laws through which the organic world has been evolved, that he is what he is.

V

To say that the world or the order of nature is reasonable is like saying how well the body fits the skin. The order of nature fits our faculties and appears reasonable to us, not because it is shaped to them, but because they are shaped to it, just as the eye is shaped to the light or the ear to the waves of sound. Nature is first and man last. Things are good to us because our constitutions are shaped to them; no absolute goodness is argued. Fluids might seem like solids to beings differently constituted. Were the laws of the physical world designed to bring about certain results, or do the results simply follow? Shall we say that the inclination of the earth's axis to the plane of its orbit is in order that there may be a change of season? or does the change of the season simply follow as an inevitable consequence? Is the air adapted to the lungs or the lungs to the air? Of course the lesser or secondary fact is always adjusted to the greater or primary fact. The structure of a bird, the mechanism of its wings and feathers, is all adapted with the nicest accuracy to the one purpose of flying, but is there anything here we can properly call design? The wing we know is the result of slow adaptation and modification, and not of anything like deliberate contrivance. God did not will that certain creatures should fly, and so proceed to make them wings and feathers. With disuse the wing disappears or becomes rudimentary. Use therefore makes the wing. What makes use? Some mysterious impulse imprinted upon the organization of which we know nothing. What I am trying to say is, there is nothing like man's ways, nothing artificial in nature,— nothing in the finite that is copied from the infinite. Will, design, purpose, are partial terms. God is all will, all purpose, — just as the sphere is all form, that is, holds all form, and yet is of itself of no form! The circle goes in all directions, and yet in no direction.

VI

Christianity amounts to little without something to back it up, without integrity of character and fealty to truth. You may put on a varnish of religion as thick as you please. If the stuff beneath is poor, is shaky or full of knots, the result is poor. Our final reliance is always upon the man himself and not upon his creed. We care little what he believes or disbelieves, so that he believe in sobriety, justice, charity, and the imperativeness of duty, so that he speak the truth and shame the devil, and I reckon it is about so with God himself. What mankind in their better selves love can hardly fail to be acceptable to him. Atheism itself, if sincere and honest, is more in keeping with the order of the world than a cowardly and lukewarm deism. Belief in Christ will not save a man; he must be saved already or he is lost, — saved by his character and conscience, or there is no material for belief in Christ to work upon. How many people we see who freely and heartily subscribe to the Thirty-Nine Articles, yet in whom we have no confidence, and with whom we want no intimate relations! And it is not because they are hypocrites; it is because they are incapable of truthfulness or manliness.

Belief is not saving, but character is. How shall

we get character, then? how deepen and fertilize the groundwork of men's natures? It cannot be done in a moment; conversion will not do it. When a man of force and integrity joins the church, the church has an acquisition; but when a slippery, inconstant, and equivocating person joins it, it has put a brick in its walls that will not stand the weather. The frosts and the rains will crumble it, and the structure be weakened.

Character is of slow growth. It cannot be made to order. The most that can be done to encourage or stimulate it is to lay the emphasis where it belongs; to insist upon things that are essential; to stop trying to convert men to a creed, but to open their eyes to a law; show them the penalties of fickleness, falsehood, intemperance, unchastity, and riotous living, not because they contravene some command or precept of the Bible, or because they endanger their chances of felicity in some other world, but because they contravene the laws through which all growth and health and wholeness come, and endanger their well-being here and now.

The preacher cannot create force and integrity off-hand in his hearer by praising force and integrity, but a great deal is gained when a love for these things is awakened. Men are made manly by an appeal to their manliness; noble sentiments are begotten by noble sentiments; when the true patriot speaks, everybody is patriotic; when the real Christian appears, everybody loves Christianity. I once heard Fred Douglass say the way to keep a man out of the mud was to black his boots, and the first step towards making a man manly is to convince him he has a capacity for manliness. Show him that religion is not some far-away thing that he must get, but a vital truth which he lives whenever he does a worthy thing.

Religion, as something special and extra, which a man may or may not have, and which is attached to certain beliefs and ceremonies, has had its day. Whatever it may have been in the past, it is no longer a power to mould men's characters and shape their lives. That a man professes religion is no longer a recommendation to him, in applying for any place in the business or political world. It does not inspire any more confidence in him as a man or as a trusted servant, but creates a certain presumption against him. He may be a wolf in sheep's clothing; watch him closely. A commonplace poet derives great advantages from the stock forms and measures which he uses; these are the garments of mighty bards; let him discard them, and his littleness and poverty will appear. So a man often hides his mean and selfish nature in loud professions of religion; let him drop these and stand upon his own merits, and we shall not be imposed upon. When such an one fails we excuse the matter by saying, "Well, it was not the fault of the religion, but of the man."

The fault is in attaching any religious value to forms and beliefs — in having any cloaks of this kind in which a scoundrel may masquerade.

If a man professes to be a legal or medical or scientific expert, and is not, he is soon found out. This is not a cloak, but a sword, and if he cannot wield it, he is soon exposed. But a man may profess Christianity to-day and rob a bank to-morrow.

Probably no honest mind ever gave its assent to the literal truth of the Thirty-Nine Articles, or to any of the various creeds, until its sympathy and its interest had been brought over by an appeal to the emotions. The creed is an after-thought; it is the terms which the conscience makes with the reason after the reason has surrendered. In assenting to it the convert thinks he is only assenting to the truth of his religion, or to the genuineness of the emotion he has experienced. Mayhap by and by, when he discovers that he has assented to a set of propositions which, standing naked and formal as they do, are divested of the spiritual warmth and magnetism, and the incentives to noble and heroic living which they had in the fervid exhortations of Paul, or in the calm sweetness of James, and which his reason alone is now to lay hold of, he is shocked and repelled, and is in danger of losing all his religion with the discovery of the unreasonableness of his creed. This is unfortunate, because the only thing real and valuable in religion, the only thing saving in it, is the emotion of Godliness, of tenderness, gentleness, purity, mercy, truth. Without these, religion is nothing but a name, and with them the assent of the understanding to a lot of formal propositions about the plans and purposes of the Eternal, about the Trinity, or the atonement, or original sin, has nothing to do. There is no connection between these things. Religion is not a matter of reason or of belief any more than poetry is.

VII

A tree is known by its fruit, and it may be objected that false ideas in religion cannot be productive of good. But false ideas are and have been productive of good. The idea of sacrifice is now looked upon as a false idea, and has long been dropped from religious rites, but with the ancients it was not a false idea, but an undoubted means of obtaining immediate communion with the life of the gods. The man who offered sacrifices was for the time being a guest of supernatural beings, and he aimed to make himself worthy to sit at their table. The fruit or animals offered up must be without spot or blemish, and the body of the priest who offered it was to be without blemish. Can there be any doubt but that a man's religious nature, his sense of sacred and invisible things, was quickened by such a ceremony? Before the victim was slaughtered wine was thrown upon its head, that it might nod in token of consent. This, too, was a false idea, since any strange liquid thrown upon the head of a sheep or heifer, and allowed to run down upon the nose and into the mouth, will cause the animal to toss its head, as if in affirmation; but this only served to clinch the belief of the sacrificer in the immediate presence of the god.

If one could only believe that the stars were so many eyes of supernatural beings looking down upon him, and beholding his every act, would he not be more careful about doing a mean thing beneath them? Yet such an idea would not be good astronomy. History is full of false or foolish ideas that have been productive of great good. In our day we should look upon an enthusiasm like that which gave rise to the Crusades as very absurd; the notion that was the parent of this great movement was undoubtedly a mistaken one, and yet it is considered that the Crusades were a good thing for Europe. Such a mighty impulse of generosity and devotion to an idea could not be otherwise than good. "He maketh the wrath of man to praise him," and the folly of man, too. Whatever creates a noble impulse or quickens our sense of the immanence of spiritual and invisible things is justified by its results, no matter how false or delusive, in itself, it may be.

The religious world of to-day looks upon polytheism as a false religion, and relatively to us and our ideas it is false. We could not be sincere in the practice of it. But was it so to the Greek? Undoubtedly the religion of Apollo has done as much for the Hellenes, some might say more than Christianity has done for the modern world. The whole culture and civilization of Greece was the legitimate outgrowth of the religion of Apollo. Can as much be said of our civilization with reference to Christianity? Grant that the oracle of Delphi was not what it pretended to be, its answers were founded upon the widest knowledge and the deepest wisdom possible in those times. As a rule, it discouraged unworthy and encouraged worthy undertakings. Moreover, Dr. Curtius says, "The oracles were sought only by those who were inwardly or outwardly oppressed and needy of help, especially by those burdened by guilt. The atonement sought from the priest could not be obtained without humiliation and self-abasement. Confession, of sin and repentance were demanded." Delphi was the heart and conscience of Greece.

It is easy to see what a power for good the ordinance of Christian baptism may have upon him who thoroughly believes in it. If, when the neophyte feels the water close over him, he really believes his sins are washed away and he is cleansed from all impurities, will he not arise a different man, a better, a holier man? The great point is to have faith.

Truly faith can work wonders. The early Christians, the apostles, and probably Christ himself labored under the delusion that the end of the world was near at hand. It was a false idea, but it added solemnity and power to their lives. "As long as this error," says Gibbon, "was permitted to subsist in the church, it was productive of the most salutary effects on the faith and practice of Christians, who lived in the awful expectation of that moment when the globe itself and all the various races of mankind should tremble at the approach of their divine Judge."

VIII

It is easy enough to say what God is not, but, ah! who can say what he is? Can he be named or defined to the intellect at all? Probably not. The burden of the old prophets' songs was that God is past finding out, — past finding out by the intellect, by the understanding. We call him an infinite and eternal Being, but in doing so we commit a solecism, we trip up our own minds. The only notion of being we can form is derived from our knowledge of man; God as a being is only an enlarged man, and to make him infinite and eternal is to contradict the fundamental idea with which we start. A being is finite; add infinity and omnipotence, and all idea of being disappears. Can we conceive of an infinite house or of an infinite inclosure of any kind?

214

No more can we conceive of an infinite being. Can we ascribe form to infinite space? No more can we ascribe personality to God.

What appears more real than the sky? We think of it and speak of it as if it was as positive and tangible a fact as the earth. See how it is painted by the sunset or by the sunrise! How blue it is by day, how gemmed by stars at night! At one time tender and wooing, at another hard and distant. Yet what an illusion! There is no sky; it is only vacancy, only empty space. It is a glimpse of the infinite. When we try to grasp or measure or define the Power we call God, we find it to be another sky, sheltering, over-arching, all-embracing, — palpable to the casual eye, but receding, vanishing to the closer search; unfathomable because intangible, — the vast power, or ether, in which the worlds float, — but itself ungraspable, unattainable, forever soaring beyond our ken. Not a being, not an entity is God, but that which lies back of all being and all entities. Hence an old writer, in his despair of grasping God, said, "God may not improperly be called nothing." Absolute being is to the human mind about the same as nothing, or no being at all, just as absolute motion is equivalent to eternal rest, or as infinite space means no space at all. Motion implies something which is not motion, and space implies lines and boundaries. Infinite being or power gives the mind no place to rest. One's thought goes

forth like the dove from Noah's ark and finds nowhere to perch.

"How can any one teach concerning Brahma?
he is neither the known nor the unknown. That
which cannot be expressed by words, but through
which all expression comes, this I know to be
Brahma. That which cannot be thought by the
mind, but by which all thinking comes, this I know
is Brahma. That which cannot be seen by the eye,
but by which the eye sees, is Brahma. If thou think-
est that thou canst know it, then in truth thou
knowest it very little. To whom it is unknown he
knows it, but to whom it is known he knows it not."

IX

Science is rubbing deeper and deeper into our
minds the conviction that creation is a unit, that
there are no breadths or chasms, that knowledge of
one thing fits in with the knowledge of all other
things and is a ground of vantage in the soul's progress in all directions. The more active a man's
scientific faculties are, the more clear ought to be
his view of the grounds of faith; and so it would
be if the grounds of faith were continuous with the
grounds of the rest of human knowledge. But they
are not, they belong to another order of things.

Poetic truth, moral truth, and all other subtle
truths are spiritually discerned also; and that there
is any other spiritual discernment than is here im-

plied, any other that is normal in kind and valid in reason, is what the natural man cannot admit. Spiritual discernment of the kind here referred to can be communicated, proof of it can be given. A man cannot counterfeit any real intellectual quality or any real power of the spirit, but the spiritual discernment of evangelical theology cannot be communicated or verified. A man says he has it, and that is all we can know about it. He says he discerns certain things to be true, but he cannot convey his mode of viewing them to us, so that we shall see them to be true also. Of course a man who has no faculty for music cannot appreciate the charm or the truth of music. No, but those who have this gift can give us proof of it.

St. Paul's power of spiritual discernment was no different in kind from that of many other men before and since his time. How did it differ from Carlyle's power of spiritual discernment, or from Schiller's, or from Plato's, or from that of Epictetus? He had no deeper insight into human nature or into the workings of men's minds or into the mysteries that shroud human life. He had great religious power, great heroism, great wisdom, a lofty spiritual nature, but it was genetically the same as that of other men. Milton did not write his poems out of his Puritanism, out of the kind of spiritual knowledge Puritans are supposed to possess. Wordsworth wrote out of the spirit of his natural religion, not out of his orthodoxy, or *un*natural religion.

Indeed, when people have written poetry or composed any other work of art out of what they have called their spiritual life alone, the product has not been such as the world wanted to see live. In any work of prose or verse, of science or philosophy, it is only such things as put us in communication with the natural, universal, and perennial that gives the work a lasting value. Things that appeal to Christians alone are soon left behind. The natural man, as much as we may profess to despise him, is the mainstay after all in religion as well as in science. Religious poetry, as such, has little value. In fact, the only thing that will *keep* a religious book at all is the salt of the natural man. If this has lost its savor, the work is shortlived. It keeps the Bible itself fresh and makes it appeal to all hearts. What does the world value in Cowper's poetry? His discernment of spiritual truths, or rather his poetic discernment of natural universal truths? The religious idolaters who throw themselves under the wheels of Juggernaut, or offer themselves as victims at the altar of sacrifice, are heroic, without doubt, yet the world does not heed and does not remember them, but it does heed and remember the three hundred Spartans who laid down their lives at Thermopylæ. This appeals to and shows the stuff of the natural man.

MEDITATIONS AND CRITICISMS

X

"In our early days," says Schopenhauer, "we fancy that the leading events of our life, and the persons who are going to play an important part in it, will make their entrance to the sound of drums and trumpets; but when, in old age, we look back, we find that they all came in quietly, slipped in, as it were, by the side door, almost unnoticed." The great men of a race or people, the real heroes and saviours, usually come upon the scene quietly and unknown. They do not even know themselves.

The remark of Schopenhauer occurred to me in thinking of the advent of Jesus. Nothing could be more natural, nothing more in harmony with universal experience, than his coming, and his life as we may read it in the Synoptic Gospels. There was no prodigy, no miracle, no sudden apparition of a superhuman being, clothed in majesty and power, as the popular expectation indicated there would be, but the Messiah came in the natural way as a helpless infant, born of human parents. Instead of a throne, there was a humble cradle in a manger.

It really enhances our notion of his merit, or if you prefer of his divinity, that he should have been rejected by his race and people, that he should have come from a town of proverbial disrepute, that he should have been meek and lowly through life, a man of sorrows, the friend of the humble and the despised, that his kingdom should not have been of this world; in fact, that he should in every way have disappointed expectation.

All this seems in harmony with the course of nature and of human life. It agrees with the truest experience. There is a sort of poetic verisimilitude about it. Indeed, if a God were to appear this is probably the way he would come. All greatest things have an humble beginning. The divine is nearer and more common than we are apt to think. The earth itself is a star in the sky, little as we may suspect it.

Had the record made Jesus suddenly appear as a great potentate, or even as a full-grown man, as the angels are represented as appearing, or had it represented him as the child of some nymph, like certain other heroes of antiquity, the fabulous character of the story would have been apparent. But he came as a man, lived as a man, and died as a man; was indeed completely immersed in our common humanity. Nothing God-like but his teachings. Even the reputed miracles become him not; they mar his perfect humanity. They belong to the conception of him as a supernatural being, and not as a man. The notion of the Immaculate Conception also jars upon our sense of the human completeness of his character. He came as the great saviours in all ages have come, and was rejected and denied in the usual way. His lot was not exceptional. His charac-

ter and mission were not exceptional, except that
he spoke more fully to our sense of the divine than
any man has before spoken.

XI

I have often asked myself, What is the merit of the
mingled feeling of admiration and approval which
we experience toward people who devoutly hold a
religious creed in the truth of which we have no
confidence? In yonder house is an aged woman
slowly dying of an incurable disease. She can no
longer rise from her bed, or even move herself without help. Her son has come from the far West to
be with her in these last days of her life. Every
morning the son reads a chapter from the Bible, and
the old Scotchwoman, lying there on her back in
her bed, holds the accustomed family prayers. Her
voice is low and feeble, but her faith is strong, her
eye is bright, and her spirit serene. Long ago she
left her native hills for this new country; now she is
about to leave this for another country in the existence of which beyond that dark ocean she has never
had the slightest doubt, nor the slightest doubt as to
the means to be employed to secure an interest there.

What is the merit of the feeling which prompts
us to say, " How touching, how beautiful!" and that
fills us with a vague regret that such a faith is impossible to us? We could not feel so in the presence
of the ancient superstitions, the bleeding victims

on the altar, or the devotee perishing in the arms of his idol. Hence our feeling, our regret, is not a tribute to sincerity alone, or to courage, or to heroism. It is mainly a tribute to the past, to the memory of our fathers who held this faith, to our mothers who distilled it into our minds in infancy, to the old creeds and institutions which have played so large a part in the culture and development of our race.

We are like the western emigrant turning to take a last view of the home of his youth and the land of his fathers. The old ties draw us, we are filled with a deep longing and regret; a little more and we would go back and abide there forever. The new world of faith, the great western world, which this generation is fast entering, and which the next generation will more completely take possession of, is indeed a new land. Those upon whom the old associations have set the deepest mark will experience the keenest homesickness. The timid, the halfhearted, the irresolute, will not go. But much of the best blood will go, is going. The majority of the most virile minds of the century have long since taken up their abode there.

And like the other emigration, the men go first; the women and children stay behind. Woman, more tender and emotional, cannot give up the old faiths; she shrinks back from the new land; it seems cold and naked to her spirit; she cleaves unto the past, and to the shelter of the old traditions. Probably the bravest among us do not abandon them without a pang. The old church has a friendly and sheltering look after all, and the white monuments in the rear of it where our kindred sleep — how eloquent is the silent appeal which they make!

But what can be done? Thou shalt leave this land, the land of thy fathers, is a fiat which has gone forth as from the Eternal. We cannot keep the old beliefs, the old creeds, if we would. They belonged to a condition of mind which is fast being outgrown.

XII

The old theology asks us to believe that the relations between God and man were radically different at some former period of history than now, that they were more intimate and personal. Is it probable that man's relation to the air, the water, the earth, has ever been any more intimate and vital than now; that his food ever nourished him in any other way than it does now, that offspring were ever begotten by any other method, or that the relations of men to each other were ever essentially any different from the present? If God is not a constant and invariable power he is nothing. Does gravity intermit? Are not the celestial bodies always on time? Are not life and death and generation always subject to the same laws? The moral and religious nature of man rises and sinks; he seems more conscious of God and of divine things in some period of history than in others, in some races than in others, but this is a fluctuation doubtless governed by natural causes, if we could penetrate them, and is not the result of any change of plan or purpose of the Eternal. God walked and talked with men in the patriarchal days, because men interpreted their own thoughts, dreams, desires, motions, as the voice of God. We define and differentiate things more nowadays, though probably the old prophets were strictly correct, for is not man himself a manifestation of God? With the devout and religious habit of mind comes the boldness to ascribe all our thoughts and promptings and happenings to God. It is the not-ourselves that rules and controls us and in which we live and move and have our being, and whether we call it God or by any other name the fact remains the same. The religious mind gives it one name, the scientific mind another; the former makes it personal and sustains a personal relation to it, the other makes it impersonal and names it law or force. Indeed, the dispute between the saint and the scientist is not as to a matter of fact, but as to a matter of feeling. One reaches through consciousness what the other reaches through intellect, and the results differ just as the media differ. There are fear, love, hope, and other emotions mingled with the one experience, but there are none of these things mingled with the other. Indeed, one is an *experience* while the other is a rational process.

XIII

The region of the unconscious in one, so much more deep and potent in some men than in others, is our hold upon the Eternal. The disclosure of thoughts, of knowledge, of power, that we did not know we possessed, — these things may be said to be from God. The Biblical writers ascribed all spontaneous thoughts to God. Such were a revelation. When these men looked deep into their hearts, they found God there and they conversed with him freely. What we call communing with ourselves, the religious mind calls communing with God. Every writer, every orator, knows what it is to see depths and views open in his mind that are a surprise to him, and that but a moment before he was ignorant of. This is inspiration. All scriptures are given by inspiration, because they come not by way of the reason and the understanding, but by way of the conscience and the spiritual sense; all poetry the same. We call it God or we call it genius, just according to our training and habit of mind. The mind does open sometimes and refuses to open at others. Undoubtedly a man has or has not a capacity for great and high thoughts. How the thoughts arise is as great a mystery to him as to another. In our speech of to-day we do not ascribe these things to God — to any objective agency or power external to ourselves; it is a purely subjective phenomenon, as much so as

THE LIGHT OF DAY

the seeing of visions or the dreaming of dreams. Mohammed thought he saw and talked with Gabriel and once with God; St. Paul believed he heard a voice and saw a light from heaven: we call these things hallucinations, the man's own conscience or fears or hopes or thoughts seen externally; but they were as real to them as any outward object.

All that lies back of our conscious powers, all the *not me*, the pious soul calls God. And indeed, how little we are in and of ourselves. Look at yonder water-wheel doing its work. All the *not me* in that case is the water that flows, and gravity that makes it flow, and without them the wheel is nothing. In our own case we draw quite as largely upon the universal, upon that which is not ourselves. Call all the *not me* God and we have some idea of the closeness and immanence of God to the old Hebrew prophet. Science shows all this *not me* to be impersonal force; it shows how much of it is race or family or climate or environment or physiology or geology; how the mind itself is a part of the body; how the conscience itself arose, how the church, the state, and all institutions. A certain order of minds stamps this force with personality. All the early minds did, but science leads us farther and farther away from an anthropomorphic God. It is singular that we should have outgrown anthropomorphism so far as to deny personality to the separate forces of nature, but ascribe it to nature as a whole.

226

XIV

The view which the old theology takes is an artificial view. It imposes upon the world arbitrary and artificial conditions, as if one were to paint the grass blue and the sky green. It says the world is a lost and condemned world; that God is estranged from the race of man; that through some act of disobedience of Adam six thousand or more years ago, sin and death entered the world, and that a way of escape from eternal ruin has been provided for mankind by the life and ignominious death of an innocent and just person, Jesus of Nazareth. This I say is an artificial view, an utterly unscientific view, — as much so as the belief not so very old that witches could cause storms and tempests, or as the view of Justin Martyr that the earth becomes fertile when dug by a spade because the spade is in the form of a cross.

Theology looks upon sin as something entirely apart from a man's natural defects, and upon religion as something entirely independent of his good qualities. Both are from without, — one the work of a malignant spirit, the other the gift of a good spirit, but both arbitrary or mechanical, and in no way related to the ordinary course of nature. How different the natural or scientific view! When we look upon the world with the eye of a philosopher, we see that it is indeed the theatre of opposite and contend-

227

ing forces, but that the good, that is the good from the point of view of the best interest of the race, is slowly triumphing. We see the race struggling up into a higher and better life ; the long, dark, and devious route which man has come is disclosed, but his evolution has gone steadily forward. We do not find sin, in the theological sense. We see defects and imperfections, we see vice and disease, the ends of nature crossed and thwarted, but no more and no differently in the case of man than in the case of the animals and plants. We see, in fact, that death is everywhere the condition of life. We do not find that the theological system takes hold of fact as reality at any point. It is a matter entirely extraneous, or apart from the laws and condition of things. There is no place for the scheme of redemption. It looks just as artificial as the Ptolemaic system of astronomy. It is an invention of theology. On our maps we paint the different states and countries different colors and make the boundaries very prominent, but in nature we know these things are not thus differentiated. The different climates are not thus sharply separated ; neither are day and night divided by right lines. But our theology is as artificial as our maps or as our division of time.

How easy to see that these systems have come down to us from an entirely different state of things, an entirely different condition of mind, from that which prevails to-day; a state of mind which viewed all things externally, in an arbitrary and artificial light, which looked upon nature as the theatre of strife between beneficent and malignant spirits, which saw satanic agencies everywhere active, which saw all forces as supernatural forces, which begat a belief in magic, divination, alchemy, astrology, witchcraft, which believed an old woman could turn herself into a wolf and devour flocks of sheep, which looked upon an eclipse or a comet, not as a natural event, but as a supernatural. Nearly all these dark superstitions have perished; the condition of mind that begat them has passed away, but the superstition of the magic of Christ's blood and all those pagan notions of heaven and hell have survived; though the intense realization of them of the old days of witchcraft is fast fading out. They are coolly held as intellectual propositions, and that is about all. The light of science, where it is fully admitted, is as fatal to them as sun to mildew. Science begets a habit of mind in which these artificial notions cannot live, just as the study of medicine begets quite a different theory of disease from that of the Indian practitioner.

The study of nature kills all belief in miraculous or supernatural agents, not because it proves to us that these things do not exist, but because it fosters a habit of mind that is unfavorable to them, because it puts us in possession of a point of view from which they disappear. The opposite of the natural man is

not the spiritual man, — for the natural man is often
the most spiritual, — but the *artificial* man, the
man upon whose mind has been foisted an artificial
system of belief, a view of things, a view not encouraged by nature, but in opposition to nature.

An artificial man, a man to whom all promptings
of nature and suggestions of reason were looked
upon as the whisperings of the evil one, — such was
and still is the good old orthodox believer. He cherished an artificial system of belief, a system which
attributed curious plans and devices to God outside
of nature, to save fallen man, — a system of belief
the most perfect expression of which is found in the
creed and elaborate ritual of the Catholic Church.
All the other churches are more or less compromises
with nature, with the natural man. They concede
some rights to him, the right of private judgment,
the most precious of all. But the Romish Church
concedes nothing ; it is the expression of absolute
outward authority; it is as arbitrary and unnatural
as anything can well be; it is the complete expression of a church, of a religious organization, of a
system of things which takes a man's salvation out
of his own hands and puts it into the hands of an
ecclesiastical hierarchy. At one extreme stands
naturalism or science, at the other stands the Catholic Church, while the other churches occupy inter-
mediate grounds. Indeed, there is a regular grada-
tion from Rome down or up to nature, the Anglican

Church probably standing nearest Rome, and the Unitarian nearest nature.

xv

I apprehend that the success of Christianity has not been owing to the fact that it is true as a system of doctrines, but that it is true as a system of ethics. It is a good working hypothesis. It restrains vice, it stimulates virtue. The doctrines are false, but they gave force, and, as it were, dramatic representation to the ethics; they embodied it in living concrete form, as in a parable or allegory, so that they have a new power over men's hearts and minds. But always have the doctrines been held as primary, and the ethics as secondary, though the two were inseparable. The orthodox churches to-day set more store by the doctrines, when the pinch comes, than by the ethics. It is more necessary to believe certain things than to be a certain type of man, to lead a certain kind of life. The American Board of Foreign Missions refuse certain candidates for labor in the foreign field who hold an extra belief in the extent of God's mercy to the heathen. If you believe in probation after death, says the board, you are none of ours, no matter what your daily walk and conversation may be.

By making the object of religion some other world, some other state of existence than this, a great leverage seems to have been gained. It gave room for the imagination to work, for the ideal to play a part. The enchantment of distance, the fascination of the unknown, the lure of the absolutely pure and perfect (which of course would not satisfy us when attained, any more than their opposite), have been great helps in elevating the race. The conscience of the race has slowly become attuned to these high promises and ideals. The present life is vulgar and mean, and to a large part of mankind seems hardly worth the having. The world of which we form a part is always more or less a prosy commonplace world; we are crushed and dwarfed by its materialism or its dull cares. Heaven must be some other world, some far-away elysian field. This hope, this lure, keeps the heart from failing. That this "poor life is all," how such a conviction would cause millions of souls to sink back into the slough of despond; because this life is poor to them, they have not the power to transform it and see it shot through with celestial laws. This earth is no star in the heavens to them, but a very vulgar and prosaic clod.

The question to be asked of a conclusion of science is, Is it true or false? We stand before a people's religion with the inquiry, Is it elevating, is it saving? We stand before poem or work of art with the inquiry, Is it beautiful, is it inspiring? We stand before a question of politics with the inquiry, Is it expedient, is it conducive to the best interests of the country? We stand before a question of morals with the inquiry, Is it right, is it good? But we always stand before a conclusion of science with the inquiry, Is it *true*?

Whether or not the Gospel records are true as history, they have wonderful, even magical power as literature. Their certitude, their good faith, their sweetness, their solemnity, their mysticism, and their aroma of the sacred and divine are almost irresistible. Only very strong minds or else very dull ones can withstand them. A spell is put upon the mind of the reader, and his logical faculties forget to assert themselves. It seems as if these things must have happened just as the Gospel writers put them down, — as if the whole order of the world, and the whole relation of man to it, and of God to man, must have been entirely different in those days from what it is now. It is a glimpse into the land of poetry and fable. We escape from the tyranny of nature, from the grossness and irreligion of the actual world, into a realm where all is plastic and beautiful and satisfying. Then the power of Christianity to inspire beautiful and disinterested lives, — is it not an old story, do we not know it well? It does not offer a system of philosophy, but a religious incentive.

When it attempts to play the rôle of interpreter of the visible order of the universe, its failure is pathetic; its proofs are childish; its science is essentially pagan; its story of the Fall as an explanation of the origin of evil, and its "plan of salvation" as a means of escape from this evil, do not, as science, rise above any of the pagan conceptions of the rationale of things.

SPIRITUAL INSIGHT OF MATTHEW ARNOLD

I NOTE that one of our religious journals looks upon Matthew Arnold as he appears in his prose writings as "singularly deficient in spiritual insight." Unless the terms are used in some special and restricted sense, I do not think the charge quite just. If it is meant that he was not eminently a devout nature, a sample of the specialization of the spiritual and religious faculties, like Newman or Maurice or even Sir Thomas Browne, then I quite agree. But if it is meant that he was deficient in the power to apprehend the value and importance of invisible, spiritual things, the value of the religious sentiment in man, that he had not a clear, penetrating vision into the sources of the spirit's wealth and strength, that he was not moved and attracted by the good as well as by the beautiful, by righteousness as well as by lucidity, then I protest. I think Arnold must be classed among the men who, like Wordsworth, Coleridge, Carlyle, Emerson, are essentially religious, men who reach and move the spirit and help forward the higher life; less than the men named in some respects, but superior in others, — superior to any of them in clearness of vision, in power to see things exactly as they are. The great army of literary men and poets are worldly minded; whatever else they satisfy, they do not satisfy our religious yearnings. Who would say that Chaucer or Spenser or Byron or Burns or Pope had any religious value? All Arnold's more notable poems sound the spirit's depths. His mind glows in presence of the great facts of life, death, and eternity. Its yearning, spiritual aspiration and penetrating insight are remarkable. It is the soul that feels and responds to them, and not merely the æsthetic and literary faculty. All deep, spiritual-minded men feel

> . . . "the heavy and the weary weight
> Of all this unintelligible world."

This burdened Matthew Arnold's soul, but it never obscured the clearness of its vision. Does our religious editor deny him spiritual insight because he refused to accept the miracles, or because he did not penetrate the mystery of the Trinity, the Atonement, original sin, and other enigmas with which the religious world has burdened itself? Who has penetrated these mysteries? Millions of pious souls accept them, and call their acceptance an understanding of them, but they confuse words. These are transcendent mysteries that baffle all reason.

It is true that in his prose writings Arnold appears

solely as the critic, the divider of one thing from another, the classifier. He is cool, clear, disinterested.
He does not so much address the religious, emotional
nature as the intelligence, and aims to satisfy that
craving in us for those things that are true and excellent in and of themselves. In his religious writings, in "Literature and Dogma," "God and the
Bible," "St. Paul and Protestantism," Arnold is still
the critic, the diagnoser; he is solely bent on seeing
things just as they are; but it seems to me there is
no want of spiritual insight, unless we narrow the
term so that it means seeing the truth of some particular creed or dogma.

When we examine our notions closely, it is very
doubtful if what is called spiritual insight differs
from any other true *insight*, — the power to penetrate into hidden forces and meanings, to get at the
true inwardness of things. True, the logical, reasoning mind differs from the imaginative poetic
mind, and from the fervid religious mind; but is
not the faculty with which we determine the truth
or falsity of a proposition the same in all cases? A
thing cannot be false to the intellect and true to
what we call the soul or the heart, nor *vice versa*.
The intellect may not see what the heart feels, but
the heart is blind, and the mind alone can supply
it with eyes. There is no more unsafe guide in our
search for the truth than our feelings or our attractions and repulsions. We feel so and so about a

matter, but the previous question is, *ought* we to feel so and so? By the term "spiritual insight" I suppose we commonly mean the capacity to apprehend spiritual things, or those things that are related to our religious needs and aspirations, and I find no clearer or fuller recognition of these things than in the pages of Matthew Arnold. The passage in one of his earlier essays from Greek poetry sets in emotional, poetic form the thought which is at the bottom of all his religious criticisms and teachings: "O! that my lot may lead me in the path of holy innocence of word and deed, the path which august laws ordain, laws that in the highest empyrean had their birth, of which Heaven is the father alone, neither did the race of mortal man beget them, nor shall oblivion ever put them to sleep. The power of God is mighty in them, and groweth not old."

No doubt there has grown up in the church a usage which assigns to the terms "spiritual insight," "spiritual-mindedness," etc., a narrow and exclusive meaning, and which would deny them to all persons who do not accept the popular view of Christianity, or who lived in the pre-Christian ages. One of the most successful so-called religious books of the day, Drummond's " Natural Law in the Spiritual World," narrows the spiritual world to the creed of the Scotch Presbyterian Church. Unless you believe this creed, you are separated from the spiritual world by the same gulf that separates the organic from the inorganic; and in the tone of the press and pulpit of the churches generally there is an assumption of usufruct of spiritual and divine things. In the creed of the true-blue Calvinistic church it is held that a person can have no insight into spiritual things till his eyes are specially opened by an act of divine grace. Then things become straight and plain to him which before were dark and crooked. This may be so, but I trust the good brethren will forgive me if I say this view represents a phase of thought which is transient and limited, and which is certainly passing away. It is one phase of Puritanism, and is fading out with the rest. How can we deny spiritual insight, spiritual-mindedness, or faith, hope, charity, to such pagans as Plato, Socrates, Marcus Aurelius, or to Plutarch or Seneca? or, in our own time and country, to such a man as Emerson, — a man, as it seems to me, of the most heroic spiritual fibre? "But Esaias is very bold, and saith, I was found of them that sought me not, I was made manifest unto them that asked not after me." Think you the man of science does not also find God? that Huxley and Darwin and Tyndall do not find God, though they may hesitate to use that name? Whoever finds truth finds God, does he not? whoever loves truth loves God? "He judged the cause of the poor and the needy: was not this to know me? saith the Lord."

Has conversion, then, no power to open the eyes?

The old-fashioned conversion of our fathers and mothers was an emotional, not an intellectual process; it was an upheaval of the conscience and not a turning over of the mind, and is impossible to most natures. It did not open the eyes, but it enlisted the heart and the feelings; it begat love. Love is not sharp-sighted, but it is creative; it finds meaning and value which an outsider does not find. A man who loves his church and its sacraments and ceremonies finds a significance and an importance in them which another does not. But it is to be remembered that these things are relative and personal, and not absolute and universal. It is love which creates them, our own heightened feelings which impart them. They are subjective phenomena, and not objective realities. The creed of our church is not any more true that we love it and find it full of meaning and beauty. There is but one truth-tester, and that is the impartial, impersonal intellect.

In all his criticism Arnold aimed at disinterestedness. He does not appear as an advocate before a jury whose passions and prejudices are to be moved, but as a pleader before the judges in the highest court, whose reason is to be convinced. Religion as a sentiment, or as an emotion of his heart, is not often present in his prose writings, but religion as a conviction of his intellect is. He states the law, and states it with just as much spiritual insight as St. Paul does, but not with the same force of conviction, because with less passion. Paul is a passionate pleader and denunciator; his words melt and burn: —

"For I delight in the law of God after the inward man: but I see another law in my members, warring against the law of my mind, and bringing me into captivity to the law of sin which is in my members. O wretched man that I am! who shall deliver me from the body of this death?"

See how dispassionately Arnold states the same law: —

"As man advances in his development he becomes aware of two lives, one permanent and impersonal, the other transient and bound to our contrasted self; he becomes aware of two selves, one higher and real, the other inferior and apparent; and that the instinct in him truly to live, the desire for happiness, is served by following the first self and not the second."

It is to be remembered of Matthew Arnold that his culture, his temper, and his method were essentially classical, Greek; that he looked with suspicion upon all disproportionate mental or spiritual development, that he would have the man equally developed on all sides of his nature, and that he says in one of his poems that he owed "special thanks" to the "even-balanced" soul of the old Greek bard, whose ideal he seems to have had ever before him,

"Who saw life steadily and saw it whole."

a different fact, proceed from different premises, and are totally inadequate to face such a deduction.

It is a source of wonder to me how modern theology has stood for so long a time the test of astronomy, — in fact, has harnessed astronomy into its service. It is not that the stars are less convincing, but that men are harder to convince than I was willing to believe. It is not difficult to see how this fantastic conception of things would fall before the standard of him who had got even the insects or the minutest fact of nature. How, then, can it prevail before him whose standard is the globe, — "round, rolling, compact," — with no possible failures, or no conceivable age, obeying no namable rule or method, yet above all rule and method, — purely an inspiration, whose vast beauty and perfection the highest speech can only edge?

Our proudest statements go but a little way — at most but recognize this as up, that as down, that as east, this as west, but absolutely, without reference to point or place, which way is east and which way west? Leave the earth behind you as a speck in the sky, and which way is up, which down? Now where is your immutable fact? Enlarge your sphere of observation a little, take into account the circle, instead of the fragment of an arc, and how relative and puerile your boasted achievements seem! It is as if sight were added after groping with the hands.

Are the great facts of science, then, only so many

all may be spoken, — all theories, literatures, arts, religions, — tried and judged. This principle shows all as parts of one plan, and makes every fact significant. Can there be any failure or miscarriage now? Because the circle is emblematical of nature is why nature will not be reduced to a point. We cannot put our hand upon this or that and say, "Here is what it is all for, — this is the end of the world." There is no end or beginning, and can be none. Tried anywhere, nature presents the same front. Every part is strong by the strength of the whole. Can you prostrate a sphere? Every point on its surface is a centre. So everywhere. The earth, we say, is forever falling into the sun and forever ceasing to fall; indicating all directions and going no direction; every point at the top, and yet no one point at the top, etc. Is this a flat contradiction? Very well, this is nature, — this is the lesson the earth teaches, and it satisfies. What is time? It is not the present moment; before you can say "Now," it is gone; and it is not the next moment, because that is not. Yet time *is*. So with the old sophists' puzzle that motion is impossible, because a body cannot move where it is, nor where it is not. Life is as impossible of explanation, — it is neither the one thing nor the other, but a constant becoming. To this principle the last analysis brings you, and the soul sees that the final explanation can never be made, — that there is no final explanation. With

246

this sight comes perfect faith. When the mind sees that the universe is self-sustained, yea, stronger than this, that there is no condition or possibility of the opposite thought, what more can be said? Now you may chant "unmitigated adoration." Now you may praise with electric voice: —

" Open mouth of my soul, uttering gladness,
Eyes of my soul, seeing perfection,
Natural life of me, faithfully praising things,
Corroborating forever the triumph of things.

" Illustrious every one!
Illustrious what we name space — sphere of unnumbered
            spirits,
Illustrious the mystery of motion, in all beings, even the
            tiniest insect,
Illustrious the attribute of speech — the senses — the
            body,
Illustrious the passing light! Illustrious the pale reflec-
            tion of the moon in the western sky!
Illustrious whatever I see, or hear, or touch, to the last."

Do we realize the amazing grandeur and beauty of the voyage we are making, — all the more grand and beautiful because on so large a scale and in so vast an orbit that none suspect it, none witness it; speeding with more than the speed of a rifle-bullet, and the fact patent only to the imagination, not to the senses? In the heavens, among the stars, separated from the nearest by measureless space, yet related to the farthest by the closest ties, upheld and nourished by a power so vast that nothing can measure it, yet so subtle that not a hair loses its place, the morning or the evening star no more favored, no more divine, these ways the eternal ways, the heavenly ways, the immutable ways, — what more would we have! Is it all a sham and a failure, then, — is it all foulness and sin?

Incorruptible and undefiled, — the soil under foot as well as the sky overhead. It fills me with awe when I think how vital and alive the world is; how the water forever cleanses itself; how the air forever cleanses itself, and the ground forever cleanses itself, — how the sorting, sifting, distributing process, no atom missing or losing its place, goes on forever and ever! Perpetual renewal and promotion! —

" Now I am terrified at the Earth ! it is that calm and
        patient,
It grows such sweet things out of such corruptions,
It turns harmless and stainless on its axis, with such end-
        less succession of diseased corpses,
It distills such exquisite winds out of such infused fetor,
It renews, with such unwitting looks, its prodigal, annual,
        sumptuous crops,
It gives such divine materials to men, and accepts such
        leavings from them at last."

Does this power with which I move my arm begin and end in myself? On the contrary, is it not the same or a part of that which holds the stars and the planets in their places? In performing the meanest act, do I not draw upon the vast force with which the universe is held together? Can anything transpire of which the Whole does not take cognizance? "Not a hawthorn blooms," says Victor Hugo, "but is felt at the stars, — not a pebble drops but sends pulsations to the sun." Be assured we are not detached, cut off, by all these billions of miles of space, but still as close and dependent as the fruit that hangs to the branch.

I cannot tell what the simple apparition of the earth and sky mean to me; I think at rare intervals one sees that they have an immense spiritual meaning, altogether unspeakable, and that they are the great helps, after all. In the open air I know what the poet means when he swears he will never mention love again inside of a house, and that he will follow up these continual lessons of the earth, air, sky, water, — declaring at the outset that he will make the poems of materials, for only thus does he hope to attain to the spiritual: